Computing Fundamentals UNIX® Systems

Douglas Troy
Miami University, Oxford, Ohio

The Benjamin/Cummings Publishing Company, Inc.

Redwood City, California • Fort Collins, Colorado
Menlo Park, California • Reading, Massachusetts • New York
Don Mills, Ontario • Wokingham, U.K. • Amsterdam • Bonn
Sydney • Singapore • Tokyo • Madrid • San Juan

This book was produced by the Benjamin/Cummings Electronic Production Department on an Apple Macintosh II with PageMaker. The output was generated on an Apple LaserWriter II NTX.

This book is in the Benjamin/Cumming's *Computing Fundamentals Series*

Series Editor: William S. Davis

UNIX is a trademark of AT&T in the USA and other countries.
IBM is a trademark of International Business Machines Corporation.
Xenix is a trademark of Microsoft Corporation.
SunOS is a trademark Sun Microsystems, Inc.
Ultrix is a trademark of Digital Equipment Corporation.
DEC is a trademark of Digital Equipment Corporation.
AIX is a trademark of International Business Machines Corporation.
SCO is a trademark of the Santa Cruz Operation.
NeXT is a trademark of NeXT Computer.

Library of Congress Cataloging-in-Publication Data
Troy, Douglas A.
    Computing fundamentals: UNIX systems/by Douglas Troy
        p.   cm.
    ISBN 0–201–19827–4
    1. UNIX (Computer operating system) I. Title.
QA76.76063T76   1990   89–77938
005.4'3–dc20   CIP

4 5 6 7 8 9 10 AL 959493

The Computing Fundamentals Series

The books in Addison-Wesley's *Computing Fundamentals Series* feature tutorials that teach the reader how to use specific software packages. Their low selling price makes them attractive as self-teaching aids and as supplements to a primary text. A unique feature entitled "What can go wrong?" anticipates problems, suggests a cause, and helps the reader recover. The modular nature of the series should prove attractive to the instructor of a microcomputer applications course. Current and planned titles include:

Concepts, Second Edition
dBASE III PLUS™
dBASE IV™
Lotus® *1-2-3*® *Release 2.01/2.2*
PageMaker® *for the IBM PC*

Microsoft® *Word*
PageMaker® *for the Macintosh*
PC-DOS & MS-DOS®
UNIX®
WordPerfect 5.0/5.1®

Another title in the series, *Productivity Tools,* introduces essential computer concepts and then teaches the fundamental skills needed to use four popular microcomputer applications: PC-DOS and MS-DOS, WordPerfect, Lotus 1-2-3 and dBASE III PLUS.

To My Parents

Preface

Computing Fundamentals: UNIX Systems is part of Addison-Wesley's *Computing Fundamentals Series*. Its purpose is to teach you how to use the UNIX operating system, one of today's most popular operating systems. Except for elementary typing skills, it assumes no prior knowledge.

There are many reasons to learn to use the UNIX operating system. You might want to learn about the capabilities of the UNIX system as a part of a study of operating systems in general. More likely, you might need to use a UNIX system because it is the operating system on the computer on which you are learning a programming language, using a database management system, or performing some other business or scientific application. In any case you want to learn about the basics of the UNIX operating system quickly and efficiently so that you can perform the work at hand.

Getting started with the UNIX system can be a difficult task. Often, the only documentation available is the UNIX manual, which is intended for use as a reference manual for experienced users. In addition, several different versions of UNIX are on the market today, each with its own subtle variations. Finally, many beginning users consider the UNIX commands somewhat cryptic.

Because of the rise in the popularity of UNIX, many books have been written about it. Most of these books concentrate on one version of UNIX and then attempt to cover nearly every command that is available for that version. Their goal is to cover UNIX as an end in itself. Because these texts try to cover so much, they tend to resemble reference books with added explanation of each command. A reader can become bogged down in the details.

This book was written to meet the needs of users who want to learn the basics of UNIX efficiently and with minimal cost. *Computing Fundamentals: UNIX Systems* does not cover every UNIX command; that is not its intent. Instead, it introduces the features you'll need to use UNIX to accomplish your particular application. In addition, the text covers the most popular versions of the UNIX system. When you finish, you will have sufficient background to read the UNIX manuals and learn additional features on your own.

Like the other books in the series, *Computing Fundamentals: UNIX Systems* is organized as a set of tutorials. Often, tutorials assume the reader will follow the instructions perfectly and that nothing will go wrong. That's unrealistic; in the real world, something always seems to go wrong, and nothing is more frustrating to the beginner than hitting a dead end. Appearing throughout this book is a unique feature entitled "What Can Go Wrong?" that anticipates problems, suggests a cause, and tells you how to recover. You should find this feature most useful.

Acknowledgments

I would like to thank Mr. William Davis, the series editor, for inviting me to write this book and for helping me to formulate the text. Comments and suggestions from the following reviewers also proved very useful: Judith Dart Boxler of Vancouver Community College, Susan R. Wallace of the University of North Florida, Joseph F. Kent of the University of Richmond, Jeff Maglich of Oxford, Ohio, Jan L. Harrington of Marist College, and Lee Jacknow of SUNY College of Technology at Farmingdale. Additional thanks go to Keith Wollman, Deborah Lafferty, and Sarah Hallet of Addison-Wesley.

DAT
Oxford, Ohio

Contents

1

Getting Started

This chapter:

- reviews the components of a computer system
- describes the purpose of an operating system
- describes types of operating systems
- introduces the UNIX operating system

Components of a Computer System

What components compose a computer system? Broadly speaking, the components are hardware, software, and data.

The **hardware** is the computer processor, its memory, peripheral devices like workstations, printers, and disk drives, and the communication paths that connect these components. Standing alone, the computer hardware can do very little useful work. Software must be added to make the computer system useful.

Software can be grouped into two categories: system programs and application programs. **System programs** are usually supplied by the computer vendor; they provide the foundation that allows users to run programs designed to solve their individual problems. Software that is designed to solve individual user's problems is called **application programs**. Examples of system programs are those that let you log onto a computer, type commands, and write programs. Application programs include word processors, spreadsheets, database software, and scientific programs such as statistical analysis programs.

The heart of a computer's system software is the **operating system** (OS). The operating system is a program that provides the interface between users of the computer and the computer hardware. This book is about a popular operating system called the UNIX operating system.

Data, the third component of computer systems, are information used or produced by the software. Data are often stored for long periods of time in the form of **files** on disk and tape drives.

Purposes and Components of an Operating System

The purposes of an operating system are to make the computer easier to use and to manage the computer's resources (disk, memory, etc.) efficiently. An operating system makes the computer easier to use by providing the environment in which a user can easily run programs. It manages resources by helping the user to store and organize files and to communicate, print, and display information. In some cases the operating system allows many users and programs to share one computer system.

Some of the major software components of a typical operating system are the following:

1. A **command interpreter**. This software initiates user commands and locates and runs programs.

2. Software to assist with **input and output** of data between programs and the computer's hardware resources.

3. A "manager" that allows more than one user or program to share the computer hardware with other users and programs.

Figure 1.1 summarizes the major components of an operating system. Figure 1.2 illustrates the major components of the UNIX operating system.

On UNIX systems the command interpreter is called the **shell**; the shell is actually both a command interpreter and a programming language. The core of the UNIX operating system is called the **kernel**; it contains both the input/output software (called drivers) and the resource management software. Many programs that are commonly needed, such as editors, compilers, and

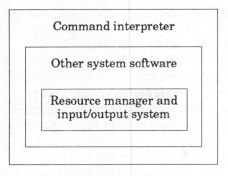

Figure 1.1 Components of an operating system.

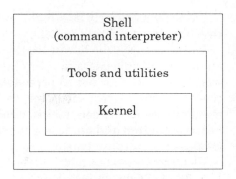

Figure 1.2 Components of the UNIX operating system.

the like, are also supplied with the operating system; these programs are often called **utilities** or **tools**. The UNIX operating system thus includes the shell, the kernel, and a collection of useful utilities and tools.

Types of Operating Systems

The goals of an operating system vary according to the user's requirements and the capabilities of the available computer hardware; thus there is a wide variety of operating systems. For example, operating systems for small personal computers, called **single-user interactive operating systems**, allow a single user to enter commands and quickly see their results. More powerful computers, called minicomputers or mainframe computers, are so fast that more than one user or program can share the system at a time. Computer systems that permit more than a single program or user to share the computer require a **multitasking or multiuser operating system**. Further, computer systems that are used to control physical pro-cesses and machinery, such as a jet plane guidance system, must be able to respond quickly to physical events. These systems utilize a **real time operating system**.

A fourth type of operating system is called **time sharing**. Time sharing combines the multiprogramming and multiuser capabilities of large computer operating systems with the interactive nature of the single-user personal computer operating system. Time sharing systems allow more than one user (or program) to share a computer and to do so on a command-by-command basis. Time sharing systems differ from real time systems in that time sharing systems are designed to work with humans, whereas real time systems are designed to work with machines. Thus time sharing systems must respond to a command in a reasonably short amount of time, but not necessarily as quickly as a real time system. The UNIX operating system is a time sharing operating system.

Until recently, the hardware used in microcomputers was incapable of allowing multiple users to share the computer's hardware. Microcomputers were best suited for use as personal computers utilizing a single-user interactive operating system. However, as the power of microcomputers has grown, the distinction between micros, minis, and mainframes has blurred, and the microcomputers and minicomputers of today have the power of the mainframes of yesterday. This means that time sharing operating systems can now operate on many microcomputers as well as minicomputers and mainframe computers. In fact, UNIX is probably the best known and most popular time sharing operating system that runs on a variety of computers.

History of the UNIX System

The name UNIX is not an acronym. It was coined in a research department at Bell Telephone Laboratories as the name for a small operating system developed between 1969 and 1970 by Ken Thompson and Dennis Ritchie. The main goal of this first version of UNIX was to provide a convenient file system to be used to store the researcher's programs and data on a Digital Equipment Corporation (DEC) computer that was comparable to today's microcomputers. In 1971, UNIX was modified to provide a time-shared, multiuser environment to support program development (for the researchers) and text processing (for the corporation). It is interesting to note that the UNIX operating system was not intended to be sold as a commercial product and was not written for a computer produced by Bell Labs. The system was intended to serve the internal needs of a group of people at Bell Labs, and it ran on a small computer that was conveniently available.

Major revisions of the UNIX system occurred in 1973 and 1975. In 1973 the UNIX system was rewritten in a programming language called C, which was developed at Bell Labs by Dennis Ritchie. The C language is independent of a particular computer, as are FORTRAN, Pascal, and BASIC. Computer programs written in languages like C and FORTRAN are said to be **portable**, that is, they can be easily modified to run on different families of computers. In 1975 the UNIX system was modified so that it operated on computers other than, and very different from, DEC computers. This was possible because most of the UNIX system was written in C, a portable language. This event was an important stage in the evolution of UNIX because it demonstrated that UNIX was a portable operating system. Today, UNIX is considered to be one of the most portable operating systems available.

The UNIX system was not actively marketed by AT&T (Bell Laboratories' parent) in the 1970s for legal reasons and because UNIX was not intended to be a commercial product. However, versions of the UNIX system were distributed to many universities, resulting in the development of many UNIX variations. The most famous and widely used variation was developed at the University of California at Berkeley.

After the divestiture of the Bell System, AT&T became more interested in marketing the UNIX system as a commercial product. Many corporations have now licensed the UNIX system and have produced their own UNIX variants. Today, versions of UNIX include

- System V, from AT&T;

- Varieties of System V such as Xenix from SCO and AIX from IBM (AIX includes some features from Berkeley UNIX);

- Berkeley UNIX, from the University of California at Berkeley;

- Varieties of Berkeley UNIX such as Ultrix from Digital Equipment, Mach from Carnegie Mellon University (used on the NeXT computer), and SunOS from Sun Microsystems.

These versions of UNIX operate variously on microcomputers, minicomputers, and even supercomputers. Although many variations of the UNIX system are available, all are based on the original work at Bell Labs and are similar in the capabilities that they provide.

Another variation in UNIX systems is that there are several popular shells (command interpreters). Two very different types of shells in use are (1) a visual shell that uses a full screen display and a pointer device like a mouse and (2) a line-at-a-time shell that uses the prompt/command line interface that is common on many time sharing systems. Many true workstations use a visual shell. Most time sharing systems connected to terminals use the line-at-a-time shell. In this text we will assume the use of one of the line-at-a-time shells.

Two of the most widely used line-at-a-time shells are the Bourne shell and the C shell. Others, such as the Korn shell, also exist. This text presents examples using both the Bourne and C shells.

Despite the variety of UNIX system versions, UNIX is considered by many to be the operating system of choice for multiuser time sharing applications. Various industry and standards groups are working to eliminate, or to at least reduce to a small number, the variety of UNIX systems on the market. Learning the basics of the UNIX system will equip the reader with the knowledge necessary to use computer systems produced by many different vendors. This text is intended do just that: teach the basics of the UNIX system.

Getting Ready

Before you turn to the first tutorial in Chapter 2, complete the checklist given in Fig. 1.3. Your computer center staff or instructor can supply you with the information needed to complete the checklist. Information includes

```
                        System Checklist

UNIX system version (System V, Berkeley, other): _____

Shell (Bourne shell, C shell, other): _____

Login id: _____     Password: _____

Erase character: _____   Kill character: _____

Interrupt character: _____

Terminal type: _____

Log off command (logout, exit, or [Ctrl] and d): _____

Printer command (e.g., lpr, lp, printer name): _____

Connection information:
(may include system network names, dial-up phone numbers, and communica-
tion parameters necessary for connection)


```

Figure 1.3 System checklist.

1. The version of UNIX (System V, Berkeley, or other).

2. The shell version.

3. Your UNIX login id.

4. Your UNIX password, if it has been assigned.

5. The UNIX system erase, kill, and interrupt characters.

6. Your log off command.

7. Information about printing files.

8. Specifics about how to connect to your system.

Record this information on the checklist. If you are working alone and cannot determine the UNIX or shell version, the kill character, or the erase character, Chapter 2 describes how to determine this information after logging into the UNIX system. Chapter 2 also explains more about the meaning of the information.

You will probably be using the UNIX system through a terminal, a personal computer (PC) emulating a terminal, or a remotely connected desktop workstation. Some readers may be using UNIX on a dedicated personal computer or workstation. For simplicity the term **workstation** is used for the keyboard/screen, whether it is a personal computer, terminal, or a true workstation.

If you are using a terminal, a personal computer, or a workstation acting as a terminal, a good starting point is to find out the name or type of terminal that you will be using. UNIX will need to know this information. For example, common terminal types are vt100 and vt220. You should get this information from your computer center staff or instructor and record it on the checklist.

Next, familiarize yourself with your workstation's keyboard. Keys that are especially important to the use of UNIX include: caps-lock, break, del (delete) or rubout, control, escape, return (or enter), /, \, |, >, <, ', and the backspace key. Unfortunately, there is no standard for the location of these keys on the keyboard. Figure 1.4 illustrates two common keyboards, one from an IBM PC and one from a terminal keyboard.

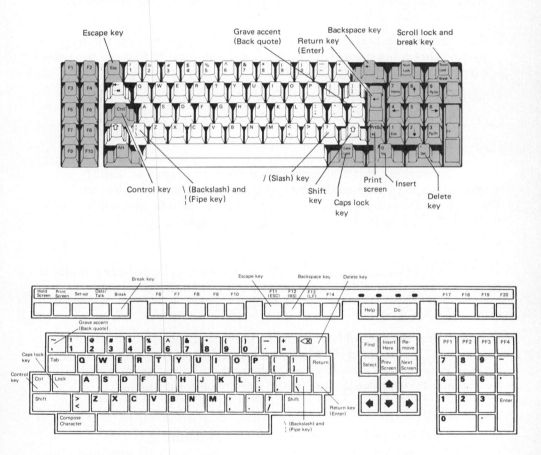

Figure 1.4 The locations of some important keys. Courtesy of Digital Equipment Corporation.

Most UNIX systems have a printer available for making hard copy (paper) listings of information. Chapter 2 discusses this in more detail. Find out from your instructor the proper command for generating listings and, if necessary, the printer name to be used if your UNIX system has more than a single printer. Record this information on the checklist.

After you have examined your workstation, you will need to find out how to connect to the UNIX system. You will probably use one of the following three alternatives:

1. The workstation may be permanently connected to the UNIX system. In this case, all you need to do is turn on the terminal if it is not already operating.

2. The workstation may be connected into a network that will allow connection to more than one computer system. In this case you will need to know the name of the UNIX system that you will be using and will need to supply this name to your network's prompt.

3. The workstation may be connected to the UNIX system over the telephone system through a modem. To connect, you will need to find out the telephone number of the UNIX system.

Determine the method of connection and record this in your checklist.

Notation

Throughout this text a consistent notation is used to identify keystrokes other than the usual letters, digits, and punctuation characters. These are called special keys. When a special key is to be pressed by itself, the key will appear in the text by itself; for example,

Del

indicates the delete (or rubout) key. If two keys are to be pressed simultaneously, their symbols will be separated by the word *and*; for example,

Ctrl *and* d

indicates that the control key should be pressed along with the letter "d." This is similar to using a shift key on a typewriter. If two keys are to be pressed in sequence (press the first, release it, and then press the second), their symbols will be separated by the word *then*; for example,

Break *then* ↵

indicates Break then Enter. Enter is also called Return.

A final convention that will be used in this text is one for specifying the format for a line-at-a-time command's syntax. The **syntax** is the rules that you follow when you enter a command.

An example of a UNIX command is the **ls** (list) command: `ls -l phonelist`

NOTE

UNIX commands are usually abbreviated to very short names. For example, ls is an abbreviation for list. Once you learn the abbreviation, the command is very easy to type!

This command can be broken down into three parts, as shown in Fig. 1.5. The three parts shown in Fig. 1.5 are:

1. The **command name**. The command name is the way you tell the UNIX system the operation or program that it should perform.

2. The **options**. The options give the command more information about exactly what you want it to do. For most UNIX commands, options begin with a dash (-) to distinguish them from arguments.

3. The **arguments**. These are the objects that the command is to operate upon. In Fig. 1.5, phonelist is the name of an inventory of telephone numbers. Thus the command in Fig. 1.5 will list information about the phonelist.

Here are some rules about these three parts of a command:

1. The *command name* must be *entered exactly as shown* in the syntax rules. Each command in the UNIX system has its own name.

2. Most commands provide a variety of *options*, which are *optional*. Options modify the way the command works. If the command suits your purpose without options, they can be skipped entirely. For other situations you might need to use one or more options with a command. However, you must select from the options given in the command's syntax. For most UNIX commands, each option is indicated by a *single character*.

3. The *arguments* are usually the names for collections of data, called **files**, that you have created. Arguments differ from the command name and the options. The command name and options are fixed; you can't change them. However, the arguments are names that *you select* on the basis of your own needs.

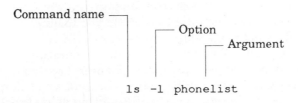

Figure 1.5 The parts of a line-at-a-time command.

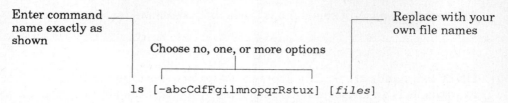

Enter command name exactly as shown

Choose no, one, or more options

Replace with your own file names

ls [-abcCdfFgilmnopqrRstux] [*files*]

Figure 1.6   Syntax for the list command with explanations.

As an example, the complete syntax for the list command is presented in Fig. 1.6. This syntax tells you that the ls command has 21 possible options and accepts one or more files for its arguments. The square brackets in the syntax are a convention that indicates something that can be skipped. The argument, *files*, is printed in a different type style to indicate that it is to be replaced by *your* file names. Based upon the above syntax, some valid ls commands are as follows:

Command	Comments
ls	no options, no arguments
ls addresses	no options, one argument
ls -a	one option, no arguments
ls -a phonelist expenses	one option, two arguments
ls -al	two options, no arguments
ls -a -l	two options, no arguments

Notice that multiple options can be grouped together (as in ls -al) or written separately (as in ls -a -l). These two examples represent the same command.

The syntax notation just described will be used in this book when each new command is introduced. It is the same as is used in the UNIX on-line and printed manuals.

A Look Ahead

The goal of this text is to present the fundamentals of UNIX that you need to accomplish your work. The intent is to help you to quickly become productive. The text does not pretend to cover every UNIX command. The UNIX system documentation, along with on-line documentation, does this.

The text is organized as a series of tutorials. Chapter 2 covers logging in and out, setting the terminal type, typing commands, and some simple file creation using the vi editor. Chapter 3 covers file editing using the vi screen editor and a few of the UNIX tools. Chapter 4 covers the UNIX file system.

Chapter 5 presents some of the most widely used UNIX tools and describes how to connect these tools together into more powerful combinations. Chapter 6 presents ideas for customizing and controlling your UNIX account. Chapter 7 presents additional vi commands; Chapter 8 describes ways to share information and communicate with other UNIX users. Chapter 9 introduces you to ways that you can take advantage of UNIX's multitasking capabilities. Chapter 10 presents an overview of UNIX shell programming. Appendix A contains a summary of vi commands and a summary of UNIX commands. Appendix B presents the answers to the self-test questions that follow each chapter.

Many tutorials assume that the reader will follow the instructions to the letter and that nothing will go wrong. This is not always true. Instructions can be misinterpreted, hardware or software might fail, or you might decide to experiment. Throughout this book, you will find sections labeled "What Can Go Wrong?" These sections anticipate common problems, explain the probable cause, and suggest how you might recover from the error condition.

We noted that there are several prominent variations in the UNIX system. In time sharing environments you will probably be using one based on AT&T's System V or Berkeley UNIX. This text is written primarily for users of a version of System V or Berkeley UNIX system using either the Bourne or C shell. Where commands vary between these two UNIX versions, we have attempted to explain the possible differences.

Summary

You'll find a summary of new UNIX features at the end of each chapter. No features were introduced in Chapter 1.

Self-Test

The answers to all self-tests are in Appendix B.

1. The purposes of an operating system are to _____ for the user and to _____ resources.
2. List four different types of operating systems. a. _____ ,
   b. _____ , c. _____ , d. _____
3. The goals of an early version of the UNIX operating system were to provide an environment for _____ for the researchers and to provide _____ for the corporation.
4. The UNIX system is a _____ operating system.
5. True or false: The UNIX system was originally developed for the commercial market.
6. The command language is provided by the UNIX _____ .

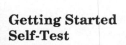

7. The core of the UNIX system is called the _____ .

8. True or false: Today, there is one single standard version of the UNIX operating system.

9. The characteristic that allows UNIX to be easily transported from one computer system to another is called _____ .

10. Consider the command syntax shown below:

    cat [-us] files

    Which of the following are valid commands based upon this syntax?

    a. cat

    b. cat birthdays

    c. cat receipts disbursements

    d. cat -us

    e. cat -s phonelist

    f. cat -u expenses income

Exercises

1. Other than the operating system, give another example of system software.

2. List two examples of applications software.

3. In what ways would a multiuser operating system such as UNIX be more complex than a single-user operating system?

4. Briefly explain how there came to be multiple versions of the UNIX operating system.

5. This chapter introduced the syntax for UNIX commands. Define the term "command syntax."

6. The following are examples of valid UNIX commands:

    ls

    ls filename

    ls -l

    ls -l filename

    ls -d

    ls -d filename

    ls -ld

    ls -ld filename

    From these examples, write the general syntax for the above command using the notation shown in Fig. 1.6.

2

Logging in and Using Commands

This chapter:

- discusses logging in and out of the UNIX system
- covers entering of commands, correcting typing mistakes, and stopping commands
- discusses setting the terminal type and the TERM environment variable
- introduces files, directories, and the vi editor
- introduces printing the contents of a file

Logging In

To begin using most UNIX systems, a user first logs in. **Logging in** is the process that permits a system to allow only authorized use of the computer. Since most UNIX systems are multiuser systems, it is necessary to permit only authorized users to log in. This is accomplished by assigning each authorized user a login id and a password. You should have obtained this information and recorded it on you system checklist (Fig. 1.3, Chapter 1).

Before you can log in, however, you must gain access via a workstation to your UNIX system. As discussed in Chapter 1, the three common ways to connect to a UNIX system are the following:

1. turn on a workstation that is permanently connected to the system;

2. using a network, enter the name of the UNIX system in response to a network request; or

3. dial into a UNIX system using the telephone system and a modem attached to a terminal or a PC emulating a terminal.

The required information, such as the name of the computer system or the telephone number, can be obtained from your organization's computer center staff or your instructor. This information should be recorded on the checklist shown in Fig. 1.3 (Chapter 1).

At this point in the tutorial you should go to your workstation and connect to your UNIX system. After you have connected to the system, the next message you see should be a response from the UNIX system giving the system name, the version, and a login request. The message should resemble that shown in Fig. 2.1. (*Note:* Some systems simply display the login: prompt.)

If you do not see the login: prompt within a few seconds, try pressing ⏎. If the login: prompt still does not appear, refer to the "What Can Go Wrong?" section below.

At the login prompt, the UNIX operating system is requesting that you identify yourself to the system. You should enter your assigned login id, *in lowercase characters*, followed by ⏎. Do this now. If you have been assigned a password, the next message that you see will be a request that you enter the password. The prompt is

```
password:
```

In response to this prompt, enter your password and press ⏎. If a password has not been assigned to you, then UNIX will not request it. Note that when you type your password, no characters will appear on the screen. This is a security precaution to prevent someone from stealing your password.

If you encounter trouble logging in, see the "What Can Go Wrong?" section below.

After you have successfully logged in, the UNIX system may greet you with a message-of-the-day, possibly a notification that you have mail, and

```
UNIX System V Release 02.01
login:
```

Figure 2.1 A typical login prompt.

14

```
The system will be shutdown for maintenance
Sunday at 8 a.m.  It will be available again at
noon on Sunday.

You have mail.
$
```

Figure 2.2 A typical response after a successful login.

finally a prompt from the shell. The prompt is usually either a $ or % charac-
ter. This prompt is your indication that you can now enter commands to be
executed by the computer. Figure 2.2 shows an example of this output.

Logging Off

Multiuser UNIX systems have an upper limit on the number of users
who can be logged in at a time. This is because of limitations of the resources,
such as the number of workstation connections, disk space, and the like.
When the upper limit is reached, no additional users can log in. Thus when
you have finished a work session on your system, you need to inform UNIX of
this fact so that the system can free the resources assigned to you and make
them available to another user. The process of informing UNIX that you are
finished is called **logging off**.

At the shell prompt, you can enter a command or you can log off of the
system. Most UNIX systems use one or more of the following commands for
logging off: Ctrl *and* d, **logout,** or **exit.** Your logoff command should be
recorded in your checklist. If you don't know which command to use, then use
Ctrl *and* d. You should now log off by entering your log off command. For
logout or exit, press ↵ after entering the command.

You should always verify that you have successfully logged off. Leaving a
terminal logged in presents a potential security problem because an unauthorized user could gain access to the system through such a terminal. To
verify your logoff, notice the system's response following the logoff command.
You should *not* see a new shell prompt. Instead, the workstation should
return to the state that it was in before you logged in. This means that you
will see one of the following responses:

1. For terminals that are permanently connected to the UNIX system you
   will see a new login: prompt displayed.

2. For terminals connected over a network you will see the network prompt.

3. For dial-up telephone access the UNIX system or the modem will hang up
   the telephone connection.

What Can Go Wrong?

Note: Read the "What Can Go Wrong?" section only if you encountered a problem.

1. After you connect to the UNIX system, garbage is displayed on the screen instead of the `login:` prompt.

Cause 1: The transmission speeds of the computer and the workstation are mismatched.

Solution: Find out from your computer center staff the correct speed and parity and have the workstation's speed changed. If the workstation is a terminal, this might involve use of the "setup" functions. If the workstation is a personal computer, the speed will be changed through the PC's software. Again, discuss this with your computer center staff.

Cause 2: Other communication parameters within the workstation are not set correctly. These may include settings known as parity or number of data bits.

Solution: See the solution to Cause 1. Your computer center staff or instructor will have to supply the correct hardware or software settings for proper communications.

2. After you enter your login id, nothing happens.

Cause: You did not press ⏎ after your login id, or your connection to the UNIX system has been disrupted.

Solution: Press ⏎. You should see some response from the UNIX system. If you see the `password:` prompt or a login message similar to Fig. 2.1, you can continue with the tutorial. If you see no response, your connection might have been disconnected; try reconnecting to your system and, at the `login:` prompt, enter your login id, *then* press ⏎.

3. After you enter your password, nothing happens.

Cause: You did not press ⏎ after your password, or your connection to the UNIX system has been disrupted.

Solution: Press ⏎ after entering the password. If you still do not see a response, try to reconnect to your UNIX system, at the login: prompt enter your login id, *then* press ⏎. At the password: prompt, enter your password *then* press ⏎.

4. After entering your login id and your password, you receive the message Login incorrect, and the login: prompt reappears.

Cause: Either your login id or your password was entered incorrectly, or you have not been given the correct login id or password.

Solution: Retry entering your login id and password. If you continue to receive the Login incorrect message, see your computer center staff or your instructor and verify the correctness of your login id and password.

5. After logging in, nearly all messages from the system are displayed in uppercase characters, each of which is preceded by a backslash character.

Cause: The caps-lock on your keyboard was on, and you entered your login id in uppercase characters. The UNIX system now thinks that your workstation is incapable of displaying lowercase characters, so it converts every lowercase character to uppercase and precedes it with a backslash to tell you that these are *really* lowercase characters.

Solution 1: Turn off the caps-lock by pressing the caps-lock key. Log off by entering your log off command (see your checklist) followed by ⏎, and log back in again, this time using lowercase characters. If your terminal does not support lowercase, you should find a new terminal because life with a UNIX system will be a lot of trouble without both uppercase and lowercase characters.

Solution 2: In System V UNIX, after logging on, enter the command:

```
stty -lcase
```

which will reset the communication link properly without logging off.

6. Nothing happens when Ctrl *and* d is pressed.

Cause 1: You might not have pressed Ctrl *and* d simultaneously. Pressing these keys independently is not the same as pressing them together.

Solution: Press Ctrl *and* d together. If this fails, the command exit or logout is supported on many UNIX systems. Try exit for System V or logout for Berkeley versions of UNIX.

Cause 2: You might not have entered Ctrl *and* d at the shell prompt.

Solution: Ctrl *and* d will log you off only when entered at the shell prompt. Be sure that the shell prompt is displayed and try again.

Cause 3: Ctrl *and* d might be disabled on your system for log off use.

Solution: Use exit, logout, or whatever log off command is in your checklist.

7. After you log on, your screen seems "frozen," and you get no response when you press keys.

Cause: You have accidentally pressed Ctrl *and* s or the "scroll lock" key. This freezes the screen.

Solution: Press the "no scroll" key again or press Ctrl *and* q. This will resume output to the screen.

Entering Commands

Before beginning this section, you must reconnect to your UNIX system and log back in, following the steps of the previous section. You should now see your shell prompt character.

At the shell prompt (usually a $ or % character), you can enter UNIX system commands. First, press ↵ a few times. With each ↵ you should see the shell prompt redisplayed. This is the shell telling you that it is ready for the next command.

Enter the following command *in lowercase:*

who

and press ↵. Your screen will appear similar to Fig. 2.3. This command shows who is logged in, from what terminal (tty) line, and the date and time

```
$who

troyd    tty01    Jan 20    13:30
bakers   tty09    Jan 20    11:21
$
```

Figure 2.3 Typical output of the who command.

18

of logging in. The term tty is a historic name for a terminal, derived from the brand name Teletype.

Notice that the UNIX shell does not act upon a command until ⏎ is pressed. As you enter characters, they are gathered into a buffer. Pressing ⏎ is the indication to the system that your command is complete.

Enter the command

```
who am i
```

and press ⏎. This is a variation on the who command that just displays login information about yourself. A UNIX user may have more than one login id, or the user may log in from different locations. This command will inform you of your login id and your terminal connection (tty) name.

If you have not been preassigned a password, you may assign one to your login id. For security, all login ids should have a password. Even if you have been preassigned a password, good security guidelines suggest that it is a good idea for users to change their initial password. To assign or change your password, enter

```
passwd
```

and press ⏎. The **passwd** command will issue further prompts. For example, if you already have a password, you will see the prompt

```
Old password:
```

If you see this prompt, enter your existing password followed by ⏎. Note that you will not see the password displayed as you enter it. This is a further security precaution. The next prompt, or the first if you had no existing password, is

```
New password:
```

At this prompt, enter your desired password and press ⏎.

For security purposes you should select a password that has at least six characters, preferably not your name or the name of a relative or close friend. Names are easy for a computer hacker to guess in order to obtain unauthorized access the system. So are names followed by a single digit. However, the password must be something you can remember.

Some UNIX systems enforce restrictions on passwords, such as requiring that they contain letters and numbers. If your system has such a restriction, it will inform you of this with additional messages. To make sure that you and the system agree on the new password, the last prompt displayed is

```
Retype new password:
```

Reenter your new password at this prompt. If the two entries for the new password agree, you will see the shell prompt displayed. This means that the command was a success. If the two entries do not match, you will see a diagnostic message, your password will be unchanged, and you will have to

```
$ passwd
Old password:
New password:
Retype new password:
$
```

Figure 2.4 Prompts from the passwd command.

repeat the entire passwd command. Figure 2.4 illustrates a typical display after using the passwd command.

If you make a typing mistake while entering a command, you can make corrections before pressing ⏎ by entering the **erase** or **kill** character. The erase character causes the UNIX system to ignore the last character that was entered; the kill character tells UNIX to ignore the last command entered. The keystrokes for these commands vary with UNIX implementations; yours should be recorded on your checklist. Typical erase and kill characters are

or ←   to erase the last character typed

@   to ignore (kill) a command

To verify your erase and kill characters, enter the command

      stty −a

followed by ⏎. You should see output similar to Fig. 2.5. Your output will be more extensive and differ somewhat from the figure. In Fig. 2.5 the erase character is Ctrl *and* h, and the kill character is Ctrl *and* u. The notation ^h is the UNIX system notation for control-h (Ctrl *and* h); similarly, ^u is the notation for Ctrl *and* u. As it turns out, control-h is actually the ← character. Your system might use different erase and kill characters, so make a note of these characters on your system checklist (Fig. 1.3, Chapter 1).

We will now examine the action of the erase character. Enter the following command, but *do not* press ⏎:

      paswd

```
$ stty −a
line = 0; speed 38400 baud;
erase = ^h; kill = ^u; intr = ^c quit = ^|; eof = ^d;
parenb −parodd cs7 −cstopb hupcl cread −clocal −loblk
$
```

Figure 2.5 Typical (abbreviated) output of the stty command.

At this point you realize that you have made a mistake entering the passwd command. You need to erase the w and the d, and then enter s, w, then d. Press *your* erase character once (# is used for illustration—use *your* erase character):

    paswd#

This would erase the d in the UNIX system's command buffer. The output on your system may differ; you might see

    paswd\d

to indicate that the d was erased, or you might see the cursor actually move backward over the deleted character:

    pasw<u>d</u>

Now press the erase character again, and the w will be removed from the buffer. Each erase character will remove another character from the buffer, right to left.

    Once the incorrect characters have been erased, the corrected version of the command can be entered. For example,

    paswd\d\wswd

may be displayed, or the new characters may simply overtype the old, as in the following when ⬅ is the erase character:

    passwd

If you want to remove a complete command from the buffer, you can erase all of the characters, but a shortcut is to use the line kill character. Many UNIX systems use the @ character to kill a line. Enter *your* kill character (@ is used in the following for illustration):

    passwd@

followed by ⏎ because we do not want to execute the passwd command again. This will cause the line to be completely ignored by the shell, and a new shell prompt will be displayed.

> ### Keystroke and Command Summary: Entering commands
>
> To enter a command at the UNIX prompt:
>
>   Enter the command, then press ⏎
>
> To correct typing mistakes:
>
>   Press: # or ⬅ or *your* erase character to erase a character
>
>   Press: @ or *your* kill character to ignore a line

Command summary:

who	see who is logged in
who am i	login id and tty of yourself
passwd	assign or change password
stty -a	view erase and kill characters

What Can Go Wrong?

1. When you enter the who command, you see the message

```
WHO: not found
```

Cause: You entered the who command in uppercase (WHO).

Solution: You must enter UNIX commands in lowercase. If the caps-lock key is turned on on your workstation, press that key to turn caps-lock off. Reenter the who command in lowercase.

2. When you enter the who command, you see a message similar to the following (*who* may be misspelled):

```
who: not found
```

Cause: Either you misspelled the command, or the UNIX system cannot find the who command.

Solution: Reenter the who command followed by ⏎. If you do not see output similar to Fig. 2.3 and you again receive the message:

```
who: not found
```

consult with your computer center staff or instructor.

3. The erase and ignore characters don't work.

Cause: The default erase and ignore characters have been altered on your system.

Solution: If the problem is with the erase character, try pressing [Ctrl] *and* h instead of [←]. If this fails, you can observe the current settings by entering the command stty −a followed by ⏎. To set the erase character, enter

```
stty erase c
```

where *c* is the desired erase character. For example, to make the backspace key the erase character, enter

```
stty erase ⊕
```

followed by ⏎. If the command works correctly, you will receive no message from the UNIX system except to see your shell prompt reappear.

4. On a video display screen the erase character doesn't backspace over erased characters.

Cause: Your UNIX account is not configured for a video display.

Solution: At the shell prompt, enter the command:

```
stty crt
```

followed by ⏎. The erase character should now backspace over erased characters.

UNIX Shells

Recall that there are two popular line-at-a-time shells: the Bourne shell and the C shell. The Bourne shell was developed by S. R. Bourne at Bell Laboratories; the C shell is an alternative shell developed at the University of California at Berkeley. Many UNIX systems have both shells available to the user and use one of them as the default. Systems derived from Berkeley versions usually use the C shell, while AT&T System V versions often use the Bourne shell. A third shell is the Korn shell. While many of the commands are the same for these shells, there are some differences. This section discusses some of the differences.

Using the Environment to Set the Terminal Type

The UNIX system is programmed to perform appropriately for a variety of workstation (terminal) types, but the system must be told the type of terminal that you have. PCs running a terminal emulator program will also emulate ("emulate" means "act as") a particular terminal type. Without knowledge of your terminal type, the UNIX system cannot lay out your screen properly for certain commands.

Information about your terminal type and other characteristics of your hardware and your UNIX account are stored in the UNIX **environment**. The environment consists of a set of **shell variables** and their values. Since the Bourne shell differs somewhat from the C shell in how the environment is used, each of the following two sections details the use of the environment for one of the shells: the first section is for the Bourne shell, and the second is for the C shell. Read the section that is appropriate for your shell.

Using the Environment: Bourne Shell

Read this section if you are using the Bourne shell. If you are using the C shell, skip ahead to the section "Using the Environment: C Shell."

You can examine the names and values of your shell variables by using the **set** command. Try it; enter

```
set
```

followed by ⏎. Figure 2.6 shows typical output from the set command for the Bourne shell.

The names along the left such as HOME, LOGNAME, and TERM are the shell variable names. By convention the Bourne shell variable names consist of uppercase letters; however lowercase letters can also be used for other shell variables. Each of these variables has a value, which is shown to the right of each name. Notice that in Fig. 2.6 the value for the TERM variable on the author's system is vt100. This indicates that the author is using (or emulating) a vt100 type terminal.

If necessary, you can modify the value of a shell variable. For example, the syntax of the commands to change the value of the TERM shell variable to your proper terminal type are

```
TERM=terminal-type ⏎
export TERM ⏎
```

where *terminal-type* is the type of terminal that you are using. The author's *terminal-type* is vt100, so the Bourne shell command

```
TERM=vt100 ⏎
```

```
$ set
HOME=/usr/acct/troyd
IFS=
LOGNAME=troyd
MAIL=/usr/mail/troyd
MAILCHECK=600
PATH=:/usr/ucb:/bin:/usr/bin
PS1=$
PS2=>
SHELL=/bin/sh
TERM=vt100
TZ=US/Eastern
$
```

Figure 2.6 Typical output from the set command, Bourne shell.

would set the variable TERM to vt100. To make the environment variable TERM available to other UNIX programs, the command

```
export TERM ↵
```

must also be entered. At this time you should use these commands to set the variable TERM to your proper terminal type if necessary.

Information about a user's environment, such as the terminal type, can be set automatically at login time by placing the appropriate commands into a login command file. Login command files are explained in Chapter 6.

This marks the end of the section on using the environment with the Bourne shell. If you do not want to read about the C shell's environment, simply skip ahead to the next section, "Stopping Commands."

Using the Environment: C Shell

The C shell has two sets of variables: **shell variables** and **environment variables**. Some of the variables in these two sets are related, as we will see.

You can examine the names and values of your shell variables by using the **set** command. Try it; enter

```
set
```

followed by ↵. Figure 2.7 shows typical output from the set command for the C shell.

The names along the left such as argv, cwd, history, home, and term are the shell variable names. By convention the C shell variable names consist of lowercase letters; however, uppercase letters can also be used for other shell

```
% set
argv  ()
cwd /sur/users/faculty/troyd
history 20
home /usr/users/faculty/troyd
mail /usr/spool/mail/troyd
notify
path (. /usr/ucb /bin /usr/bin )
prompt %
shell   /bin/csh
term vt100
user troyd
%
```

Figure 2.7 Typical output from the set command, C shell.

variables. Each of these variables has a value, which is shown to the right of each name. Notice that in Fig. 2.7 the value for the term variable on the author's system is vt100. This indicates that the author is using (or emulating) a vt100 type terminal.

You can examine the names and values of your environment variables on Berkeley versions of UNIX by using the **printenv** (print environment) command. Enter

    printenv ⏎

Figure 2.8 shows typical output from the printenv command. The names along the left are the environment variable names, and the values to their right are the values associated with those names. Notice that the value of the variable TERM in Fig. 2.8 is vt100.

The C shell automatically takes the value of the shell variables term, path, and user and stores these values into the environment variables TERM, PATH, and USER, respectively. For example, changing the value of the shell variable term will automatically change the value of the environment variable TERM.

To change the value of a shell variable such as the term, you use the set command. The syntax is

    set term=*terminal-type* ⏎

where *terminal-type* is the type of terminal that you are using. The author's *terminal-type* is vt100, so the C shell command

    set term=vt100 ⏎

would set the variable term to vt100, and the environment variable TERM would also be automatically changed to vt100. At this time you should use the set command to set the variable term to your proper terminal type if necessary. (*Note:* You can modify environment variables directly using the C

```
% printenv
HOME=/usr/acct/troyd
SHELL=/bin/csh
USER=troyd
MAIL=/usr/mail/troyd
PATH=:/usr/ucb:/bin:/usr/bin
SHELL=/bin/sh
TERM=vt100
%
```

Figure 2.8 Typical output from the printenv command.

shell **setenv** (set environment) command. Since changing term with the set command automatically changes TERM, setenv is not needed in this tutorial.)

Information about a user's environment, such as the terminal type, can be set automatically at login time by placing the appropriate commands into a login command file. Login command files are explained in Chapter 6.

Stopping Commands

If a command's output takes longer than you care to wait, or if a program just will not quit running, the command or program can be stopped by pressing the **interrupt** character from the keyboard. The particular character varies with UNIX implementations. The most common interrupt character is Del, while some systems use Ctrl *and* c (control-c, also denoted ^c). Pressing the interrupt key will stop most programs and return the user to the shell command prompt.

To determine your interrupt character, look at your system checklist. You can verify your interrupt character by entering the command

    stty -a

The output should resemble Fig. 2.9.

Look at your output and locate the entry intr = ^c; This is the interrupt character setting. In Fig. 2.9 the interrupt character is Ctrl *and* c (^c). Your interrupt might be different.

To experiment with the interrupt character, enter the partial command shown below, but *do not* press ⏎:

    set term

Now press *your* interrupt character (Ctrl *and* c is used for illustration):

    Ctrl *and* c

The cursor should move to the next line, and the shell prompt should be redisplayed.

```
$ stty -a
line = 0; speed 38400 baud;
erase = ^h; kill = ^u; intr = ^c quit = ^|; eof = ^d;
parenb -parodd cs7 -cstopb hupcl cread -clocal -loblk
$
```

Figure 2.9 Typical (abbreviated) output of the stty command.

If a command has been entered and ⏎ has been pressed, then the command will be running. The interrupt key will also stop a running command and return to the shell prompt, as illustrated above.

Keystroke and Command Summary: UNIX shells

To interrupt a command:

Press: *Your* interrupt character. Examples are Del or Ctrl *and* c.

Command summary:

printenv	displays environment for Berkeley UNIX
set	displays the shell variables and values
TERM=*terminal-type*	for Bourne shell, sets *terminal type*
export TERM	for Bourne shell, stores shell variable TERM into the environment
set term=*terminal-type*	for C shell, sets *terminal type*
stty -a	displays setting for interrupt character

What Can Go Wrong?

1. The interrupt character does not function properly.

Cause: Your interrupt character is different from the usual Del. On some systems the interrupt key is Ctrl *and* c.

Solution: Try Ctrl *and* c. If this does not work, discuss the problem with your system administrator.

2. After entering: TERM=terminal-type, you received the message TERM=terminal-type: not found. (The word *terminal-type* is to be replaced with the name of your terminal.)

Cause: You entered a Bourne shell command to a non-Bourne shell.

Solution: Enter the command set term=*terminal-type* ⏎, where *terminal-type* is to be replaced with the name of your terminal.

3. After entering set term=*terminal-type*, the system responds: set: not found.

    Cause: You entered a C shell command to a non-C shell.

    Solution: Enter the commands TERM=*terminal-type* ⏎ export TERM ⏎. (The word *terminal-type* is to be replaced with the name of your terminal.)

Creating and Printing Files

Types of Files

A file on the UNIX system is simply a named collection of information, usually stored on hard disk media. Files are used to hold data and programs. Files must be created by software, since humans can't directly read and write on disk drives. Files can hold information that is readable by humans, called **text files**, and files can hold data that is readable only by programs, called **binary files**. In this chapter we will introduce the use of one of the UNIX editors to create text files; the next chapter will continue this discussion.

Creating a File with vi

The program that is used to create files of text is called an **editor**. Most UNIX systems have two editors:

    ed   A line-oriented editor for hard copy terminals

    vi   A screen-oriented editor for video displays

Most users have a video display terminal, so the vi editor is frequently the editor of choice.

    The syntax required to start the vi editor is

    vi [*options*] *filename*

In this syntax, vi is the name of the editor—you must use this name to start vi. The *options* are rarely used by beginners, so we will defer discussion of them. The *filename* is the name of a new or existing file that is to be created or modified, respectively. You are free to select names for your files.

    Let's use vi. If you have logged out, go back to the workstation and log back into your UNIX system. Now, to create a new file named "probes," enter the following command at the shell prompt:

    vi probes

and press ⏎.

If the terminal type is properly set, vi will clear the screen, initialize each line with a tilde (~), and position the cursor at the top of the screen. Figure 2.10 illustrates the initial vi screen. The tildes (~) indicate nonexistent lines, which are not the same as lines that contain blanks. The cursor should be positioned at the upper left-hand corner of the screen.

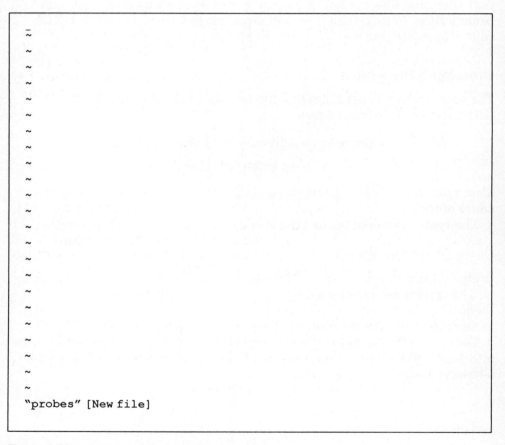

Figure 2.10 vi screen for a new file.

The vi editor is now in **command mode**. In command mode, most of the keyboard keys represent editing commands. To insert text into the file, you must put vi into **insert mode** by entering the **insert command**. Once in insert mode, most of the keys that you press will cause the corresponding characters to be entered into the file. Keys that do not cause a character to be stored are editing keys such as the erase key and, on some versions of UNIX, the arrow keys that can be used to move the cursor around the screen.

We will enter the insert command and then enter three lines of information into the file. Each line will contain information about unmanned space probes that were launched in the 1950s. First, press

    i

to enter insert mode. (*Note:* Do not press ⏎!) Now enter the first line into the file by typing

    `Pioneer 1:Moon:US`

followed by ⏎. This indicates that Pioneer 1 was launched to the Moon by the United States. The three categories of information in this line are called **fields**. The colon that separates each field is called a **delimiter**. (The use of the colon is a convention. Other characters could have been used instead.)

If you make a typing mistake while entering the the line, use the erase key to back up over incorrect characters and overtype the correct text. Enter the next line by typing

    `Pioneer 4:Moon:US`

followed by ⏎. In similar fashion, enter the line

    `Lunik 1:Moon:USSR`

Don't press ⏎ this time. The screen should now appear as shown in Fig. 2.11.

After you have entered information into vi, you must instruct vi to save the data to disk. Until you tell vi to save the data, they are not permanently stored on disk but are kept in temporary memory. To tell vi to save the file, you must return to command mode. We will do this now. Press

    `Esc`

(This is the escape key.) The cursor will move left one space, over the R in USSR. (*Note:* If you accidentally pressed ⏎ after the last word in the file, you will have a blank line in the file. You will learn how to delete this line in the next chapter.)

Once you are out of insert mode, press the colon key:

    :

The cursor will be positioned at the bottom left-hand corner of the screen, as shown in Fig. 2.12. This line is called the vi **command line**.

```
Pioneer 1:Moon:US
Pioneer 4:Moon:US
Lunik 1:Moon:USSR_
~
~
~
~
~
~
~
~
~
~
~
~
~
~
~
~
~
~
"probes" [New File]
```

Figure 2.11 Sample vi screen.

The command line is reserved for entering certain vi commands. Now enter

wq

followed by ⏎. The w means **write to disk**, and the q means **quit**. This command will save your file, display a message similar to

"probes", [New File] 3 lines, 54 characters

then exit vi, and return control to the shell. vi has many more commands than i (insert) and wq (write and quit). These will be presented in the next chapter.

```
Pioneer 1:Moon:US
Pioneer 4:Moon:US
Lunik 1:Moon:USSR
~
~
~
~
~
~
~
~
~
~
~
~
~
~
~
~
~
~
:_
```

Figure 2.12   vi command line (lower left corner).

Keystroke and Command Summary: Creating a file with vi

To create a file using vi:

  Enter: *vi filename* ⏎

vi command summary:

i	Press i to enter insert mode
Esc	Press Esc to leave insert mode
:	Press : to go to the command line
wq ⏎	Enter wq ⏎ at the command line to save the file and quit

What Can Go Wrong?

1. After you enter "vi probes," the following message appears:

```
I don't know what kind of terminal you are on - all I
have is "unknown".
[Using open mode]
"probes" [New file]
```

Cause: The TERM (for Bourne shell) or term (for C shell) shell variable is not set for your terminal type.

Solution: First, exit vi by entering

```
:q!
```

followed by ⏎. The : causes vi to move the cursor to the command line, and the ! tells vi to exit immediately without saving the file. Next, determine your terminal type by asking your computer center staff, and, after logging in but before typing vi, enter:

TERM=*terminal-type* ⏎   for Bourne shell, followed by

export TERM ⏎   for Bourne shell

set term=*terminal-type* ⏎ for the C shell

Now reenter the vi probes command, followed by ⏎.

2. After you enter "vi probes," strange characters appear on the screen.

Cause: The TERM or term shell variable is set to the wrong terminal type.

Solution: See the solution to problem 1 above.

3. While in insert mode, you press a special key such as an arrow key or backspace key, and garbage characters are inserted into your file.

Cause: These special keys send control characters to the system, and vi treats them as data.

Solution: Exit insert mode by pressing Esc. Exit vi by pressing

```
:q!
```

followed by ⏎. This command exits vi without saving the data. Now start the session over and avoid pressing any special keys. The next chapter explains how to correct typing errors without starting over from scratch.

4. When you try to exit vi by entering the command :wq, vi does not exit, but these characters are inserted on the last line of the file.

Cause: You did not exit insert mode before entering :wq.

Solution: Press the erase character three times to back up over the :wq. Now press (Esc). Now enter

> :wq ⏎

vi should exit properly.

Introduction to Directories

We have just used vi to create a file of text called "probes." If you are using this text in a course with other users, there are probably many different files called "probes" on the UNIX systems disk space. How does UNIX keep these files, all with the same name, organized? The answer is that the UNIX system manages the space on the disk drive and keeps track of each user's files by maintaining a unique **directory** of files for each user.

To get a list of the names of the files in your own directory, enter the ls (list) command at the shell prompt as follows:

> ls

followed by ⏎. You should see the "probes" file name in the list with, possibly, other files installed for you when your directory was created.

The ls command is an example of a UNIX tool. The UNIX operating system has many tools that you can use to manipulate files. Another tool is a program called **cat**, which can be used to display the contents of a file on your screen. At the shell prompt, enter

> cat probes

followed by ⏎. You should see the contents of the "probes" file displayed on your screen. (*Note:* cat is more general than was just described. It will be discussed further in Chapter 5.) Your screen should now resemble Fig. 2.13.

> **Keystroke and Command Summary: Introduction to directories**
>
> UNIX command summary:
>
> cat *filename*   to display the contents of a file
>
> ls   to list files in your directory

```
$ ls
probes
$ cat probes
Pioneer 1:Moon:US
Pioneer 4:Moon:US
Lunik 1:Moon:USSR
$
```

Figure 2.13   Typical screen after entering of the ls and cat commands.

What Can Go Wrong?

1. The ls command lists files in addition to the "probes" file.

Cause: Additional files (or directories) may have been installed for you when your UNIX account was created.

Solution: These additional files will be discussed in subsequent chapters. For now, ignore them.

Printing Files

Multiuser UNIX systems usually have one or more printers that are shared by the users of the system. Some workstations may also have a locally attached printer.

Most UNIX systems use one of the following two commands to send the contents of a file to a shared printer: the **lpr** command or the **lp** command. The lp command is common on System V versions of UNIX; the lpr command is common on Berkeley systems. The command for your system should be recorded in your system checklist.

To obtain a hard copy (paper) listing of your "probes" file, you enter your print command along with the name of the file to be printed. At this time, print your probes file by entering (lpr is used below; use your print command if it is different):

        lpr probes

followed by ⏎. If this command is operational, you will receive no message, but you should see the shell prompt reappear. If you received a message such as lpr: not found, or some other diagnostic message, try the alternative print command, such as (lp is used here for illustration):

        lp probes

and press ⏎. If this command silently returns with the shell prompt, then the command is operational.

NOTE

Some UNIX systems have more than one shared printer. To designate a particular printer, use the command

        lp -dprinter-name filename

or

        lpr -dprinter-name filename

where *printer-name* is the name of the designated printer. You must obtain the name of the printer from your instructor or computer center staff and record this information on your checklist.

To retrieve a hard copy listing from a shared system printer, you will have to inquire at your computer center or ask your instructor where listings (printouts) are distributed. Go there and pick up your listing after completing this chapter.

For workstations with attached printers, some UNIX systems support the command

    lprint *filename*

which will print the contents of the given file on the local printer. If your workstation has an attached printer, ask your instructor or computer center staff for instructions about the proper use of your printer and the associated UNIX commands.

Keystroke and Command Summary: Printing files

lpr *filename*	print the contents of the file on the system printer (Berkeley)
lp *filename*	print the contents of the file on the system printer (System V)
lpr -d*printer filename*	print the contents of the file on the specified system printer (Berkeley)
lp -d*printer filename*	print the contents of the file on the specified system printer (System V)
lprint *filename*	print the contents of the file on a locally attached printer (some versions of UNIX)

What Can Go Wrong?

1. Both the lpr and lp commands return with diagnostic messages indicating that they are not operational.

Cause: These commands are not installed on your system.

Solution: Ask your computer center staff or your instructor about the proper way to generate hard copy listings.

2. You go to the distribution point for listings, and you cannot find your printout.

Cause: Your listing might be backed up behind a long listing, or the printer operator might not have removed the listing from the printer.

Solution: Ask the operator when you can expect to receive your listing.

| Command Summary

UNIX Keystroke Summary

Ctrl *and* d or exit or logout	logoff
← or #	character erase
Del or Ctrl *and* c	stop a command during execution
@	line kill character

UNIX Command Summary

cat *filename*	display a text file on the screen
exit	logoff on some systems
logout	logoff on some systems
lpr *filename*	print the specified file (Berkeley versions)
lp *filename*	print the specified file (System V versions)
lprint *file*	print the specified file on a local printer (some versions of UNIX)
ls	list the files in a directory
passwd	change (or assign) your password
printenv	display the environment (Berkeley versions)
set	display shell variables and values
set term=*type*	set the term shell variable (C shell)
stty -a	examine settings of the erase, kill, and interrupt characters
TERM=*type*	set the TERM shell variable (Bourne shell)
export TERM	make TERM available to other programs (Bourne shell)
vi *filename*	create or edit a text file
who	display logged in users
who am i	display information about your login

vi Command Summary

Esc	leave insert mode
i	enter insert mode
:	go to the command line
:wq	write the file and quit (from the command line)
:q!	exit vi immediately without saving the file

Self-Test

1. True or false: Every user on a UNIX system must have a password.
2. The command to change a password is _____ .
3. The keystroke used to kill (ignore) an entire line is _____ .
4. True or false: The UNIX system is case sensitive.
5. The keystroke or command used to log off is _____ .
6. List the names of the two popular UNIX shells.
7. The terminal type is stored in TERM or term. These are examples of _____ variables.
8. The keystroke used to interrupt a command is _____ .
9. To create a text file, a user would usually use a program called an _____ .
10. The vi editor has two modes: _____ mode and _____ mode.
11. True or false: The user must tell vi, by using a command, to save the data in a file.
12. The names of your files are organized into a _____ . *hierarchy of directory*
13. The _____ command will list names of a user's files.
14. The _____ command is used to display the contents of a file.
15. The _____ command is used to print a file on the UNIX system's printer.
16. The _____ command is used to list the names and values of all of the shell variables.

Exercises

1. There are at least two examples in this text in which letters that you type on the keyboard are not displayed on the screen. State two such examples.
2. Contrast the operation of the kill character with that of the erase character.

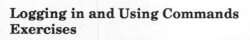

3. The vi editor uses insert mode and command mode to distinguish between keystrokes that are data and those that are commands. State another approach that could have been used to distinguish data from commands.

4. Using vi, create a telephone directory file giving the name and phone number for five of your friends or relatives. Use one line for each person. Separate the two fields of each line with a colon. After you have saved your file, display it on the screen and print a copy of the file on your printer.

Editing Files with the vi Editor

This chapter:

- introduces file manipulation commands
- introduces vi commands to add text to a file
- introduces vi commands to modify and delete text
- introduces UNIX commands to list file names and their contents

In Chapter 2 you learned how to log in, log out, and create a text file using the vi editor. You also learned that the names of your files are recorded on disk in a directory. This chapter continues the investigation of the vi editor and its use for creating and editing text files.

You might have noticed that commands that are entered at the shell prompt are always terminated by pressing ↵. From this point on, when a shell command is presented, we will state the command, such as *vi probes*. You should now assume that you must press ↵ after each command unless otherwise specified in the tutorial.

Let us use the vi editor to modify a file. First log into your system and set the TERM or term shell variable to the proper terminal type if this was necessary in Chapter 2. This is done as shown below, according to your shell type:

Bourne Shell		C Shell

```
TERM=terminal-type        or      set term=terminal-type
export TERM
```

where *"terminal-type"* is to be replaced with the name of your terminal.

Moving the Cursor

From your work in Chapter 2 you have a file named "probes" that contains information about unmanned space probes launched in the 1950s. In this chapter you will edit this file and add a new field to each line of the file: the year that each probe was launched. The launch year for Pioneer 1 was 1958; both Pioneer 4 and Lunik 1 were launched in 1959. Since we know that the file "probes" contains only probes from the twentieth century, we will add only the year in that century (58 and 59) for each launch.

To edit the file "probes," enter the command

```
vi probes
```

vi should display the contents of the file as shown in Fig. 3.1.

```
Pioneer 1:Moon:US
Pioneer 4:Moon:US
Lunik 1:Moon:USSR
~
~
~
~
~
~
~
~
~
~
~
~
~
~
~
~
~
~
~
~
~
~
"probes" 3 lines, 54 characters
```

Figure 3.1   Editing an existing file with vi.

Keystroke	Cursor Movement
j	Down one line
k	Up one line
h	Left one character
l	Right one character

Figure 3.2 vi commands that move the cursor.

The cursor should be positioned at the upper left-hand corner of the screen under the P in *Pioneer*. To add 58 to the end of the first line of the file, you must first position the cursor at the end of that line. The keystrokes in Fig. 3.2 are the vi commands to position the cursor.

Some workstations and versions of vi also permit use of the arrow keys for cursor movement. However, these keystrokes do not work for all UNIX systems; therefore this text will use the universally supported commands listed in Fig. 3.2.

Now press l (lowercase "ell") 16 times, until the cursor is on last character of the first line (the S in US). The screen should appear as shown in Fig. 3.3.

```
Pioneer 1:Moon:US
Pioneer 4:Moon:US
Lunik 1:Moon:USSR
~
~
~
~
~
~
~
~
~
~
~
~
~
~
~
~
~
~
~
~
~
"probes" 3 lines, 54 characters
```

Figure 3.3 The screen after positioning the cursor.

Notice that you *do not* press ⏎ after vi commands; vi acts on an editing command as soon as the keystroke is pressed.

You are now ready to append information to the first line of data. If you have had no problems, proceed to the next section. Otherwise, review the following "What Can Go Wrong?" section.

Keystroke and Command Summary: Moving the cursor

To edit an existing file using vi:

   Enter: vi oldfile

Vi command summary:

   j   move cursor down one line

   k   move cursor up one line

   h   move cursor left one character

   l   move cursor right one character

Unix command summary:

   vi oldfile   to edit an existing file

What Can Go Wrong?

1. When you enter vi to edit the existing file, the following message appears:

```
I don't know what kind of terminal you are on – all I
have is "unknown".
[Using open mode]
"oldfile"
```

Cause: The TERM (for Bourne Shell) or term (for C shell) shell variable is not set for your terminal type.

Solution: First, exit vi by entering

   :q!

followed by ⏎. The : causes vi to move the cursor to the command line, and the ! tells vi to exit immediately without saving the file. Next, determine your terminal type by asking your computer center staff, and, after logging in (if necessary) but before typing vi, enter one of the following two sets of commands as appropriate for your shell. End each line by pressing ⏎.

Bourne Shell	C Shell
`TERM=`*terminal-type* or	`set term=`*terminal-type*
`export TERM`	

The *"terminal-type"* is the name of your terminal or workstation (e.g., vt100). Now reenter the command `vi probes`, followed by ⏎.

2. After you enter `vi probes`, strange characters appear on the screen.

    Cause: The TERM or term shell variable is set to the wrong terminal type.

    Solution: See the solution to problem 1 above.

3. After you enter `vi probes`, vi responds with a screen of all tildes, and the line "`probes`" `[New file]` appears at the bottom of the screen.

    Cause: Either you misspelled the file name (probes) in Chapter 2 or you misspelled it in the vi command in this chapter.

    Solution: Exit vi by entering the vi command

    `:q!`

followed by ⏎. Now verify the name of the file in your directory by entering

    `ls`

at the shell prompt. If you do not see a file name resembling "probes," then you should return to Chapter 2 and recreate the file by following that portion of the tutorial. If you see the name but it is misspelled, you can change the name of the file by entering the command

    `mv `*misspelled-name*` probes`

where *"misspelled-name"* is to be the name of the file shown on your screen. End this command by pressing ⏎. The mv command is explained further in Chapter 4.

Adding Text to a File

After positioning the cursor to the end of the line, you are ready to add another field to the line. You will first enter a colon (the delimiter) and the year of the launch. To do this, you need to enter insert mode. However, if you press the command i, you will begin inserting *before* the S. Since you need to "append" characters *after* the S, you must enter insert mode using the **a** (append) command. Do this now; press

     a

followed by

     :58

(don't press ⏎). If you make a typing error, you can use the erase key to move the cursor back and reenter corrections. This completes the first line of text, and the screen should appear as shown in Fig. 3.4.

    To edit the second line of the file, you must again position the cursor. Since you are currently in insert mode, you *cannot* use the cursor movement keys— vi would simply insert the letter h, j, k, or l into your file. Instead, you must first exit insert mode by pressing the escape key. At this time, press

     Esc

The cursor should move under the 8 on the first line.

NOTE

The concept of vi's command mode and insert mode is likely to be the hardest part about using vi. A common annoyance with vi is forgetting that you are in insert mode, pressing vi command keys (such as j, k, h, and l), and having these characters inserted into your file.

```
Pioneer 1:Moon:US:58_
Pioneer 4:Moon:US
Lunik 1:Moon:USSR
~
~
~
~
~
~
~
~
~
~
~
~
~
~
~
"probes" 3 lines, 54 characters
```

Figure 3.4 The screen after editing of the first line.

Now move the cursor down one line by pressing j one time. Notice that the cursor is positioned at the end of the second line. Again enter insert mode by using the append command. Press

    a

and enter the year field:

    :59

Now exit insert mode by pressing

    Esc

The screen should appear as illustrated in Fig. 3.5.

Now enter the year field on the third line of the file. First, position the cursor by pressing j one time. Next, enter insert mode using the append command by pressing a, and enter the text:

    :59

Then leave insert mode by pressing Esc.

```
Pioneer 1:Moon:US:58
Pioneer 4:Moon:US:59
Lunik 1:Moon:USSR
~
~
~
~
~
~
~
~
~
~
~
~
~
~
~
~
~
~
~
~
"probes" 3 lines, 54 characters
```

Figure 3.5 The screen after editing of the second line.

Now save the file and exit vi. To do so, press

```
:wq
```

followed by ⏎. vi will respond with the message

```
"probes" 3 lines, 63 characters
```

and return to the shell prompt.

At the shell prompt, enter

```
ls
```

to ascertain that you have a "probes" file in your directory. Enter the command

```
cat probes
```

to verify the contents of that file.

> **Keystroke and Command Summary: Adding text to a file**
>
> Vi command summary:
>
> | a | enter insert mode but add data after the cursor |
> |---|---|
> | j | move cursor down one line |
> | l | move cursor right one character |
> | Esc | exit insert mode |
> | :wq | save the file and exit vi |
>
> UNIX command summary:
>
> | ls | list file names in the directory |
> |---|---|
> | cat *file* | display the contents of a file |

What Can Go Wrong?

1. When you attempted to move the cursor after editing the first line of data, the command (l or j) was added to the file, and the cursor did not move.

Cause: You did not properly leave insert mode and return to command mode

Solution: To exit insert mode, press Esc. You can now use the cursor movement commands to move the cursor. To remove extraneous characters from a line, position the cursor over the incorrect character and press the vi command **x**, which deletes a character. Deleting characters and lines is explored further in the next section.

Inserting, Deleting, and Replacing

To illustrate some important vi editing commands, we will create a file of probes launched in the 1960s. At the UNIX shell prompt, enter the command

```
vi probes.60
```

The screen should appear similar to Fig. 3.6.

Put vi into insert mode by pressing

```
i
```

and enter the following text (remember that you can use the erase key to correct typing mistakes if you catch them on the line with the cursor):

```
Ranger 7:Moon:US:64
Mariner 4:Mars:US:64
Venera 3:Mars:USSR:65
Pioneer 5:Moon:US:65
Surveyor 1:Moon:US:66
Lunar Orbiter 2:Moon:US:66
Luna 13:Moon:USSR:66
```

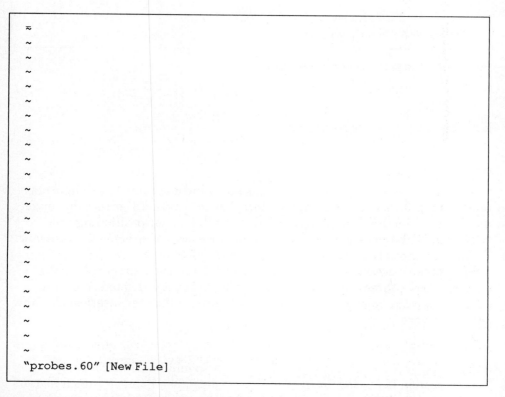

Figure 3.6 The vi screen for the new file "probes.60."

```
Ranger 7:Moon:US:64
Mariner 4:Mars:US:64
Venera 3:Mars:USSR:65
Pioneer 5:Moon:US:65
Surveyor 1:Moon:US:66
Lunar Orbiter 2:Moon:US:66
Luna 13:Moon:USSR:6̲6̲
~
~
~
~
~
~
~
~
~
~
~
~
~
~
~
~
~
"probes.60" [New File]
```

Figure 3.7   The vi screen after inserting initial text.

Now leave insert mode by pressing

[Esc]

The screen should now resemble Fig. 3.7.

We must now modify the data because they include some faulty information. Venera 3 was launched not to Mars, but to Venus. To correct this error, move the cursor over the M in Mars by using the cursor positioning commands; press k to move up a line and h to move left a character as necessary. The screen should now appear as shown in Fig. 3.8.

Now press x. Notice that the x command deletes the character over the cursor. Press x three more times until the word Mars is deleted. With the cursor under the colon that preceeds USSR, press i to enter insert mode. Now enter the word

Venus

and press [Esc] to exit insert mode. The screen should look like Fig. 3.9.

A correction is needed for the next line of data. The Pioneer launch in 1965 was Pioneer 6, not Pioneer 5. One way to correct the mistake is to use the procedure followed above when Mars was deleted and replaced with Venus.

50

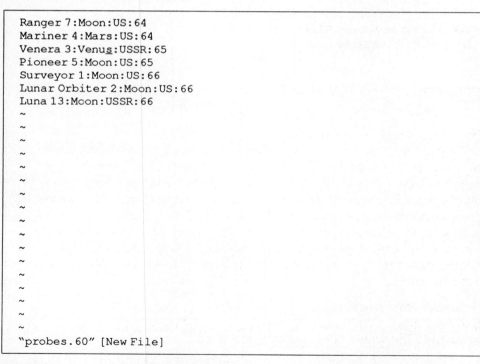

```
Ranger 7:Moon:US:64
Mariner 4:Mars:US:64
Venera 3:Mars:USSR:65
Pioneer 5:Moon:US:65
Surveyor 1:Moon:US:66
Lunar Orbiter 2:Moon:US:66
Luna 13:Moon:USSR:66
~
~
~
~
~
~
~
~
~
~
~
~
~
~
~
~
"probes.60" [New File]
```

Figure 3.8   Preparing to change Mars to Venus.

```
Ranger 7:Moon:US:64
Mariner 4:Mars:US:64
Venera 3:Venus:USSR:65
Pioneer 5:Moon:US:65
Surveyor 1:Moon:US:66
Lunar Orbiter 2:Moon:US:66
Luna 13:Moon:USSR:66
~
~
~
~
~
~
~
~
~
~
~
~
~
~
~
~
"probes.60" [New File]
```

Figure 3.9   Corrected text for Venera.

Editing Files with the vi Editor
Inserting, Deleting, and Replacing

51

However, for single-character corrections a shortcut is available. First, move the cursor under the 5 in Pioneer 5. Use j to move the cursor down, and use h to move it to the left as required. Now press

r

followed by 6. The **r** (replace) command will overwrite a single character *without* entering insert mode. The screen should appear as shown in Fig. 3.10.

In 1966, Pioneer 7 was launched to the Sun. To enter this information, you need to add a new line to the file. First, position the cursor on the line for Lunar Orbiter 2 by pressing j twice. Now press

o

(uppercase "oh"), and vi will open a new line above the cursor (between Surveyor 1 and Lunar Orbiter) and will also enter insert mode. Enter the text:

```
Pioneer 7:Sun:US:66
```

```
Ranger 7:Moon:US:64
Mariner 4:Mars:US:64
Venera 3:Venus:USSR:65
Pioneer 6:Moon:US:65
Surveyor 1:Moon:US:66
Lunar Orbiter 2:Moon:US:66
Luna 13:Moon:USSR:66
~
~
~
~
~
~
~
~
~
~
~
~
~
~
~
~
~
"probes.60" [New File]
```

Figure 3.10 The screen after correcting Pioneer 6.

```
Ranger 7:Moon:US:64
Mariner 4:Mars:US:64
Venera 3:Venus:USSR:65
Pioneer 6:Moon:US:65
Surveyor 1:Moon:US:66
Pioneer 7:Sun:US:66
Lunar Orbiter 2:Moon:US:66
Luna 13:Moon:USSR:66
~
~
~
~
~
~
~
~
~
~
~
~
~
~
~
"probes.60" [New File]
```

Figure 3.11 The screen after inserting Pioneer 7.

followed by [Esc]. The screen should appear as shown in Fig. 3.11, and vi should be back in command mode.

Let's finish this decade of information. Move the cursor to the last line of the file by pressing j twice. Press

    o

(lowercase "oh") to open a new line below the cursor, and enter the following text:

```
Venera 4:Venus:USSR:67
Surveyor 5:Moon:US:67
Surveyor 6:Moon:US:67
Pioneer 8:Sun:US:67
Pioneer 9:Sun:US:67
Luna 17:Moon:USSR:68
Venera 5:Venus:USSR:69
Mariner 6:Mars:US:69
```

and press [Esc]. The vi editor should now be in command mode. The updated screen is illustrated in Fig. 3.12.

```
Ranger 7:Moon:US:64
Mariner 4:Mars:US:64
Venera 3:Venus:USSR:65
Pioneer 6:Moon:US:65
Surveyor 1:Moon:US:66
Pioneer 7:Sun:US:66
Lunar Orbiter 2:Moon:US:66
Luna 13:Moon:USSR:66
Venera 4:Venus:USSR:67
Surveyor 5:Moon:US:67
Surveyor 6:Moon:US:67
Pioneer 8:Sun:US:67
Pioneer 9:Sun:US:67
Luna 17:Moon:USSR:68
Venera 5:Venus:USSR:69
Mariner 6:Mars:US:69
~
~
~
~
~
~
~
~
"probes.60" [New File]
```

Figure 3.12 Probes in the 60s.

A final correction to the information is necessary. Luna 17 was launched in 1970, so we should delete this line from the file. To do this, move the cursor to that line by pressing the k command twice. With the cursor anywhere on the Luna 17 line, press

> d *then* d

(this is the **dd** command). The line will be deleted, and the screen will appear as shown in Fig. 3.13.

Now save the file and exit vi by pressing

> :wq

followed by ⏎. You will see a message similar to "probes.60" [New File] 15 lines, 326 characters, followed by the shell prompt.

```
Ranger 7:Moon:US:64
Mariner 4:Mars:US:64
Venera 3:Venus:USSR:65
Pioneer 6:Moon:US:65
Surveyor 1:Moon:US:66
Pioneer 7:Sun:US:66
Lunar Orbiter 2:Moon:US:66
Luna 13:Moon:USSR:66
Venera 4:Venus:USSR:67
Surveyor 5:Moon:US:67
Surveyor 6:Moon:US:67
Pioneer 8:Sun:US:67
Pioneer 9:Sun:US:67
Venera 5:Venus:USSR:69
Mariner 6:Mars:US:69
~
~
~
~
~
~
~
~
~
"probes.60" [New file]
```

Figure 3.13 Corrected probes in the 60s.

Keystroke and Command Summary: Inserting, deleting, and replacing

Vi keystroke summary

dd	delete a line
h	move cursor left
i	enter insert mode before the cursor
j	move cursor down
k	move cursor up
Esc	exit insert mode, return to command mode
O	insert a line above the cursor
o	insert a line below the cursor
r	replace a character
x	delete a character
:wq	position to the command line, write the file to disk, and exit vi

What Can Go Wrong?

1. While in insert mode, you press a special key such as an arrow key or backspace key, and garbage characters are inserted into your file.

Cause: These special keys send control characters to the system, and vi treats them as data.

Solution: Exit insert mode by pressing Esc. Position the cursor over the incorrect data and delete it by using the x command. If an entire line is in error, delete it by using the dd command. (The dd command is explained further below.)

2. When you press the o or O command, a line is opened in the file, but the cursor is not positioned on that line but is positioned elsewhere in the file.

Cause: The cursor positioning function was not carried out correctly by the system. This could be due to some data communications incompatibility between the UNIX system and the workstation.

Solution: Press Esc to leave insert mode. Press

Ctrl *and* l

This command tells vi to repaint the screen. Use the cursor positioning commands to move the cursor to the blank line, then press

i

to enter insert mode. Enter the desired text and leave insert mode by pressing Esc.

Undo Command

For practice, create a file called "probes.70" by entering the command:

```
vi probes.70
```

at the UNIX command line. Now with the vi initial screen displayed, press i to put vi into insert mode. Enter the following information about probes launched in the 1970s:

```
Venera 7:Venus:USSR:70
Luna 17:Moon:USSR:70
Mars 2:Mars:USSR:71
Mariner 9:Mars:US:71
Luna 19:Moon:USSR:71
Pioneer 10:Jupiter:US:72
```

```
Venera 8:Venus:USSR:72
Pioneer 11:Jupiter:US:73
Mariner 10:Venus:US:73
Viking 1:Mars:US:75
Voyager 2:Jupiter,Saturn:US:77
Voyager 1:Jupiter,Saturn,Uranus:US:77
```

and press

to leave insert mode. Your screen should appear as illustrated in Fig. 3.14.

Use the cursor positioning commands and x, i, a, and r commands to make any corrections. When you are satisfied with your data, position the cursor under the 1 in Voyager 1 on the last line. This is illustrated in Fig. 3.15.

Now press x to delete the 1. To replace the 1 (since it is supposed to be there), press u. This is the undo command, which will undo your previous

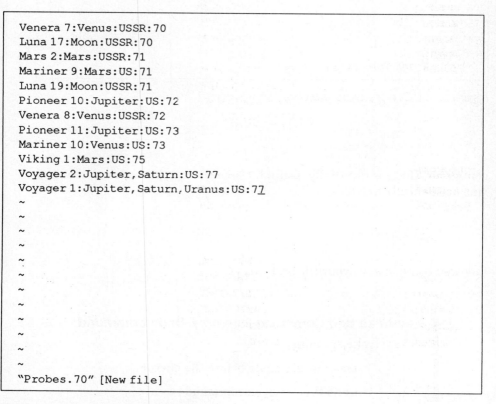

Figure 3.14   Probes launched in the 70s.

```
Venera 7:Venus:USSR:70
Luna 17:Moon:USSR:70
Mars 2:Mars:USSR:71
Mariner 9:Mars:US:71
Luna 19:Moon:USSR:71
Pioneer 10:Jupiter:US:72
Venera 8:Venus:USSR:72
Pioneer 11:Jupiter:US:73
Mariner 10:Venus:US:73
Viking 1:Mars:US:75
Voyager 2:Jupiter,Saturn:US:77
Voyager 1:Jupiter,Saturn,Uranus:US:77
~
~
~
~
~
~
~
~
~
~
~
"Probes.70" [New file]
```

Figure 3.15   Cursor positioned over 1 in Voyager 1.

command. Undo is especially useful for recovering a line or character that was accidentally deleted.

Press

    :wq

followed by ⏎ to save your file and exit vi.

> **Keystroke and Command Summary: Undo command**
> vi keystroke summary
>
>   i   enter insert mode before the cursor
>
>   u   undo the previous command
>
>   x   delete a character

What Can Go Wrong?

1. When you press the u command, the deleted character is not replaced.

Cause: You entered another command after deleting the character.

Solution: Replace the 1 by pressing i followed by 1 and Esc. Now try the exercise again.

This concludes Chapter 3. At this time you should log off of your UNIX system and review your understanding of the material in this chapter by reading the command summary and completing the self-test at the end of the chapter.

| Command Summary

vi Keystroke Summary

a	enter insert mode after the cursor
dd	delete a line
h, j, k, l	cursor movement commands
i	enter insert mode before the cursor
Esc	exit insert mode, return to command mode
O	insert a line above the cursor
o	insert a line below the cursor
r	replace a single character
u	undo the previous command
x	delete a character
:wq	position to the command line, write the file to disk, and exit vi

UNIX Command Summary

cat *filename*	display a text file on the screen
ls	list the file names in the current directory
set term=*type*	set the terminal type (C shell)
TERM=*terminal-type*	set the terminal type (Bourne shell)
export TERM	make the terminal type available to other programs
vi *file*	edit a file using vi

Self-Test

1. Below is a list of editing operations. Give the vi command to perform each of the operations.

vi command	*Function*
a. _____	delete an entire line
b. _____	delete a single character
c. _____	enter insert mode before the cursor
d. _____	enter insert mode after the cursor
e. _____	leave insert mode
f. _____	move the cursor up a line
g. _____	move the cursor down a line
h. _____	move the cursor to the command line
i. _____	open a line above the cursor and insert
j. _____	open a line below the cursor and insert
k. _____	undo the previous command

2. Four of the vi commands that you have used thus far will cause vi to enter insert mode. List these four commands.

3. You have just accidentally deleted a line of your file. What command could you enter to restore that line?

4. One way to correct a single typing mistake in vi is to delete the errant character, enter insert mode, enter the correction, and then exit insert mode. State the vi shortcut command for this operation.

Exercises

1. List the vi command(s) that you have used that require that ⏎ be pressed to activate them.

2. If you have already created the telephone directory file by completing Exercise 4 in Chapter 2, you should now do Exercise 3. Otherwise, use vi to create a telephone directory file giving the name and phone number for five of your friends or relatives. Use one line for each person. Separate the two fields of each line with a colon. Save the file and exit vi. Now do the following exercise.

3. Using vi, edit your telephone directory file and add the street address to each line in the file. Use a colon as the field separator. After changing the file, print a copy of it on your printer.

4

Organizing Files

This chapter:

- introduces file manipulation commands

- examines directory creation and use

- introduces file name expansion using wildcard characters

In Chapter 2 you learned that the names of your files are stored on disk in a directory, and in Chapter 3 you learned to utilize vi to create and edit your files. Most UNIX systems assign a separate directory for each individual user. The collection of all of the directories is called the **file system**. This chapter will further explore the UNIX file system and the manipulation and examination of text files. You will learn how to use the file system to organize your files, and you will learn how to use several UNIX tools to examine and manipulate your files.

Remember that to activate a command entered at the shell prompt, you must press ⏎. This is not explicitly stated, but is assumed, for the commands in this chapter.

Creating and Using Subdirectories

You already know that individual users on UNIX systems have individual directories that hold their files. Thus if several people are following these tutorials on your system, there are several "probes," "probes.60," and "probes.70" files on the system, but these files are organized into individual directories on the disk drive.

The UNIX file system is organized into a hierarchy, or tree structure, of directories. The top-level directory is called the **root directory**. It is specified by the single character: /. The root directory contains files and other directories, called **subdirectories** or child directories. For example, a portion of a typical UNIX file system, starting at the root directory, is shown in Fig. 4.1.

Notice that *bin*, *usr*, and *etc* are subdirectories of the root directory. The directory *acct* is a subdirectory of *usr*, while the directories belonging to two users, *troyd* and *bakers*, are subdirectories under the *acct* subdirectory. The root, /, is called the **parent directory** of the subdirectories *bin*, *usr*, and *etc*. The *acct* directory is the parent directory of *troyd* and *bakers*. Notice that directories can contain both subdirectories and files. For example, the root contains the file *unix* in addition to the above mentioned subdirectories. Also, the terms directory and subdirectory are relative terms; every directory shown in Fig. 4.1 except the root is a subdirectory of some other directory.

Certain directories are used by the UNIX operating system to organize its files. For example, the directory "/bin" holds many of the utility and tool programs.

A file is fully identified in the file system by giving its complete **pathname**. The complete pathnames for the "probes" files under "troyd" and "bakers" are

    /usr/acct/troyd/probes
    /usr/acct/bakers/probes

The / character is used to separate directory names within a pathname.

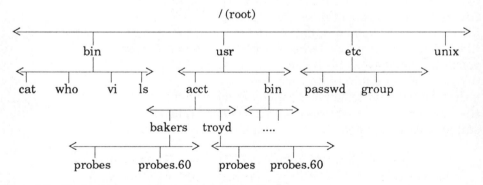

Figure 4.1 Typical hierarchical directory structure.

At this time, go to your workstation and log into your UNIX system. Set the TERM or term variable if this was necessary in previous chapters.

When you log in, you are assigned an initial **current working directory**. This is the directory that holds your own private files. You can view your working directory's path by entering the shell command **pwd** (print working directory). Enter

```
pwd
```

You will see your directory's complete pathname displayed on the screen.

Most users organize their files by creating subdirectories within their initial working directory. New directories are created by using the **mkdir** (make directory) command. Let us do this. Create a directory called "launches" to hold your space probe files. Enter the mkdir command:

```
mkdir launches
```

This command creates an empty subdirectory named *launches* under your current working directory.

NOTE

The mkdir command illustrates a characteristic of many UNIX system commands: Many commands (like mkdir) do not display screen output when successful. Most of the commands introduced in this chapter behave this way. If you do see a message displayed after entering mkdir, see the "What Can Go Wrong?" section.

Keystroke and Command Summary: Creating and using subdirectories

Summary of UNIX Commands

mkdir *directory-name*	create a subdirectory under the current working directory
pwd	print the current working directory pathname

What Can Go Wrong?

1. When you enter the mkdir command, the system responds with the message

```
mkdir: not found
```

Cause: The UNIX system could not locate the mkdir command.

Solution: Contact your computer center staff or your instructor. Ask them to check your search path.

2. When you enter the mkdir command, the system responds with the message

```
mkdir: cannot create
```

Cause: Your current working directory is configured such that you are not permitted to create a subdirectory.

Solution: Contact your computer center staff or your instructor. Ask them to check the permissions and ownership of your directory.

Copying, Moving, and Removing Files

One way to put your files into the "launches" subdirectory is via the **cp** (copy) command. There are several forms of the cp command:

cp *oldfile newfile*	copy *oldfile* to *newfile*
cp *oldfile directory*	copy *oldfile* into the directory; the copy has the same file name
cp *oldfile directory / newfile*	copy *oldfile* into the *directory* and give the copy the name *newfile*

At this time you should enter the command

```
cp probes.60 launches
```

This command will make a new copy of "probes.60" in the "launches" subdirectory. If the cp command is successful, the UNIX system will give no direct confirmation but will return with the shell prompt. If a message is displayed on the screen, it is an indication of a problem (if you received a message, see the "What Can Go Wrong?" section). Your screen should resemble Fig. 4.2 after you enter the mkdir and cp commands.

Since you now have two copies of the "probes.60" file (the original in your initial working directory and another in the "launches" subdirectory, you can

```
$ mkdir launches
$ cp probes.60 launches
$
```

Figure 4.2 A typical screen after entering mkdir and cp.

remove, or erase, the original copy by using the **rm** (remove) command. Enter the following:

```
rm probes.60
```

This will remove the original "probes.60" file but not the copy in the launches subdirectory.

The "copy and remove" scenario followed above can be combined into one step by using the **mv** (move) command. To illustrate, move your "probes.70" file into the "launches" subdirectory by entering the command

```
mv probes.70 launches
```

This command leaves a single copy of "probes.70" in the "launches" subdirectory.

As with the cp command, the mv command has several variations:

mv *oldfile newfile*	rename *oldfile* to *newfile*
mv *oldfile directory*	move *oldfile* into *directory*
mv *oldfile directory / newfile*	move *oldfile* into the *directory* and at the same time rename it to *newfile*

To illustrate the third form of the mv command, you will simultaneously change the name of the "probes" file to "probes.50" and move it into the "launches" subdirectory. Enter the command

```
mv probes launches/probes.50
```

This command simultaneously moves the file named probes from your initial working directory into the "launches" subdirectory and changes its name to "probes.50."

The complete sequence of commands that you have entered thus far should leave your screen resembling Fig. 4.3. You now have your three "probes" files

```
$ mkdir launches
$ cp probes.60 launches
$ rm probes.60
$ mv probes.70 launches
$ mv probes launches/probes.50
$
```

Figure 4.3 A typical screen of commands.

```
$ cd launches
$ ls
probes.50    probes.60    probes.70
$
```

Figure 4.4 A typical list of files in the "launches" subdirectory.

("probes.50," "probes.60," and "probes.70") in your "launches" subdirectory. This can be verified by making the "launches" subdirectory the current working directory. To do this, you use the **cd** (change directory) command. Enter

> cd launches

and use the **ls** command to list the files in the "launches" directory:

> ls

The output should correspond to Fig. 4.4. (The output of the ls command on some UNIX systems may list the file names vertically, not horizontally as shown in Fig. 4.4.)

> ### Keystroke and Command Summary: Copying, moving, and removing files
>
> Unix command summary:
>
> | | |
> |---|---|
> | cd *newdirectory* | change the current working directory |
> | cp *oldfile newfile* | make another copy of a file, giving the new file's name |
> | cp *oldfile directory* | make another copy of a file with the same name in a subdirectory |
> | ls | list file names in the current directory |
> | mv *oldfile directory* | move a file into a subdirectory |
> | mv *oldfile directory / newfile* | move a file into a subdirectory and rename the file |
> | rm filename | erase (remove) a file |

What Can Go Wrong?

1. When you enter the command

```
cp probes.60 launches
```

you receive the message

```
cp: cannot access probes.60
```

Cause: The copy command cannot find the probes.60 file.

Solution: Verify that you have correctly spelled the file name in the cp command by reentering the command cp probes.60 launches. If you receive no message, the command worked. If you get the same message again, enter the ls command to see if the file "probes" is in your directory. If it is not in the directory, return to Chapter 2 and recreate the file and update it with the information from Chapter 3.

2. The ls of the launches subdirectory does not show the files "probes.50," "probes.60," and "probes.70."

Cause: Most problems in this section will result from typing mistakes. For example, entering the command

```
mv probes.70 launch
```

is an error because the *es* is missing from the subdirectory launches. However, the command is completely valid, resulting in the file probes.70 being renamed to launch.

Solution: Examine the contents of the launches subdirectory and your home directory using the ls command. If files are incorrectly named, you can rename them using the appropriate mv or cp commands. You can verify the contents of the files by using the cat command. (The next section tells how to return to your home directory.)

Removing Subdirectories

To return back to launches' parent directory, enter the command

```
cd ..
```

NOTE

This command is cd *then* a space *then* two consecutive periods.

The .. is a UNIX convention that means "the current directory's parent."

```
$ cd ..
$ mkdir temp
$ ls
temp
$ rmdir temp
$ ls
$
```

Figure 4.5 Removing a subdirectory (typical output).

An empty directory can be removed when it is no longer of use. To illustrate this, create another directory called *temp* by entering the mkdir command

    mkdir temp

Verify its existence by entering the ls command

    ls

and you should see temp displayed on the screen. Now remove this directory by entering

    rmdir temp

Verify that temp has been removed by entering ls and viewing the output. The output from this sequence of commands should resemble Figure 4.5.

As a safety measure, if you try to remove a directory that contains files, you will receive a message from the rmdir command telling you that the directory is not empty, and the directory will not be removed.

Keystroke and Command Summary: Organizing files

Unix command summary:

cd ..	change the current working directory to the parent directory
ls	list subdirectory and file names in the current directory
mkdir directory	create a new subdirectory
rmdir directory	remove (delete) an empty subdirectory

File Names

It is good practice to select names for your files and directories that are descriptive of their contents. However, the UNIX system does not enforce this. You may use any character in your file and directory names except the "/," since that character is used to separate directory names in pathnames. You should also avoid starting a file name with a hyphen ("-"), since this character is used to indicate options in many UNIX commands. The maximum number of characters that you can use for a name depends upon your UNIX variant. Many System V versions allow up to 14 characters in a name. New versions of Berkeley UNIX allow up to 256 characters in a name. To determine whether or not your system allows more than 14 characters, change directory (cd) into your launches subdirectory by entering

```
cd launches
```

and then enter the command

```
cp probes.50 a-very-long-file-name
```

followed by the command

```
ls
```

If you see a file named *a-very-long-fi* then your system only allows up to 14 characters (the rest of the file name was ignored). In any case, names longer than 14 characters are unusual, since most UNIX users avoid excess typing! Now remove that long file by entering the following remove command

```
rm a-very-long-file-name
```

Many users on UNIX systems use a file naming convention of *filename.extension* for certain files. The *extension* is the part of the file name to the right of the period and is used to indicate the contents of the file. Some examples of extensions are:

.c   C language programs

.o   Compiled (object) programs

.doc   Text documents

We used the extensions .50, .60, and .70 on our probes files to indicate the decade.

Aside from conventions involving extensions, you are free to select appropriate names for your files.

Using File Name Wildcards in UNIX Commands

The UNIX shell provides a mechanism for generating a list of file names that match a particular pattern. Let's examine this feature. Your current working directory should be "launches" if you performed the previous section about file names. To verify this, enter

```
pwd
```

If the final name in the path is not *launches*, then cd into "launches" by entering the command

```
cd launches
```

Now make a copy of the file "probes.50" by entering

```
cp probes.50 decade.50
```

You now have four files in your "launches" subdirectory.

Now suppose that you want to know the names of all of the files in this directory that begin with the letter p. Enter

```
ls p*
```

This command tells the shell to list any file that begins with p and ends with anything else. The * wildcard means any string of characters.

NOTE

There are no spaces in wildcard patterns. For example, the pattern p* cannot have a space between the p and the *.

Your output from the ls command should resemble Fig. 4.6. (Your system might list the file names vertically instead of horizontally.)

The * is one example of a file name wildcard character. The list below explains this and other file name wildcard characters.

```
$ ls p*
probes.50    probes.60    probes.70
$
```

Figure 4.6 Typical output of the ls p* command.

*	matches any string of characters, including an empty string
?	matches a single character only
[...]	matches any of the enclosed characters. A pair of characters separated by a minus sign represents a range of characters.

Let's try the other wildcard characters. Enter the command

```
ls [a-d]*
```

which lists the names of all files that start with the letters a through d. The output should be the file name "decade.50." Another way to write this command is

```
ls [abcd]*
```

Enter the command

```
cat *50
```

which will cause the cat command to output to the screen all files that end with the character sequence 50 ("decade.50" and "probes.50") The output from these commands should resemble Fig. 4.7.

Enter the command

```
rm d?????.50
```

This command will remove all files with nine-character names that start with d and end with the sequence .50. This will remove the file "decade.50."

```
$ ls [a-d]*
decade.50
$ ls [abcd]*
decade.50
$ cat *50
Pioneer 1:Moon:US:58
Pioneer 4:Moon:US:59
Lunik 1:Moon:USSR:59
Pioneer 1:Moon:US:58
Pioneer 4:Moon:US:59
Lunik 1:Moon:USSR:59
$
```

Figure 4.7 Using file name wildcards.

Keystroke and Command Summary: File names, wildcards, and UNIX commands

File names:

    Maximum length   14 or 256 characters, depending on the version of the UNIX operating system.

Shell file name wildcard characters:

    In a file name:

    *   matches any string of characters

    ?   matches any single character

    [...]   matches a character in a list or range of characters

UNIX Command Summary

cat *filenames*	concatenate the contents of the named files and output the result to the screen
cd *subdirectory*	change the current working directory
cp *file1 file2*	copy *file1* to *file2*
ls *filenames*	list the given *filenames* if they are in the current working directory
pwd	print the current working directory
rm *filenames*	remove the specified *filenames*

What Can Go Wrong?

1. The use of a wildcard in a command does not reveal the expected result.

    Cause 1: Either you are not in the directory that you think you are in or your file names are misspelled.

    Solution: Verify your current working directory by entering

        pwd

If necessary, change into the desired directory by entering either

        cd launches

to change into launches or

        cd ..

to change from launches to the parent directory. Now verify the contents of the directory by entering the ls command. If filenames are misspelled, use mv or cp to change their names.

Cause 2: You entered a space in the pattern. The commands:

    ls p *

and

    ls p*

are *not* the same.

Solution: Reenter the command but with no spaces embedded in the pattern.

This completes Chapter 4. At this time, log off of your system and test your understanding of the topics in this chapter by completing the end-of-chapter self-test.

Command Summary

UNIX Command Summary

cat *filenames*	concatenated the contents of the named files together and display the result on the screen
cd *directory*	change the working directory to the specified subdirectory of the current directory
cd ..	change the working directory to the parent of the current directory
cp *oldfile newfile*	copy a file
ls	list the file names in the current directory
ls *filenames*	list the given file names if they are in the current working directory
mkdir *directory*	create a new subdirectory
mv *oldfile newfile*	move (rename) a file
pwd	display the current working directory
rm *filenames*	remove (erase) the specified files
rmdir *directory*	remove (erase) an empty subdirectory

Shell File Name Wildcards

In a file name:

*   matches any string of characters

?   matches any single character

[...]   matches a list or range of characters

Self-Test

1. Write a UNIX command to perform the following functions:
   a. Create a new directory named "homework." *mkdir homework*
   b. Copy the file "lab1" into the homework directory. *cp lab1 homework*
   c. Copy the file "lab1" to "oldlab1" in the current directory. *cp lab1 oldlab1*
   d. Move the file "oldlab1" into the homework directory. *mv oldlab1 homework*
   e. Change the working directory to "homework." *cd homework*
   f. Display the current working directory pathname.
   g. Delete (erase) the file "oldlab1." *rm oldlab1*
   h. From the "homework" directory, change the current working directory back to its parent directory.

2. Give the complete path name for the file "passwd" shown in Fig. 4.1. */etc/passwd*

3. The top-level directory in the UNIX file system is called the __root__ directory.

4. Give a UNIX command that would perform the following:

   a. Print all files in the current working directory whose names end with the digit 5.

   b. List the names of all files that consist of only four characters and start with the letter s.

   c. Remove all files whose names end with the two character sequence .o.

   d. Using the cat command, display all files that end with a single digit (i.e., 1 through 9).

5. The maximum number of characters permitted for a filename on your version of UNIX is _____.

6. Multiple choice: Using the file name convention filename.extension, the extension is used to:

   i. Complete the required part of every file name

   ii. Give information about the contents of the file

   iii. Make the name longer if it is too short

   iv. Indicate the names of subdirectories

74

Exercises

1. Give the written word in English that describes the following commands

   cp

   rm

   mv

   mkdir

   rmdir

   cd

2. If you completed Exercise 2 or Exercise 3 in Chapter 3, you should now make a subdirectory called "phone" and *move* (not copy) your telephone directory file into that subdirectory.

3. After completing Exercise 2, make the "phone" subdirectory the current working directory. Print a copy of your telephone directory from that subdirectory.

5

UNIX Tools and Utilities

This chapter:

- illustrates input/output redirection
- introduces several new UNIX tools and filters, including cat, sort, grep, pr, wc, pg, and more.
- describes how tools can be connected into more powerful combinations
- shows how to use the on-line manuals to get help

One of the important contributions of the UNIX system to the development of operating systems has been the concept of the software "toolbox." This concept holds that an operating system should provide the user with a set of simple tools (programs) along with ways to combine the tools to perform more complicated tasks. This chapter examines the toolbox approach.

Input and Output Redirection

The UNIX system has many programs that can be used to process files. The philosophy of the UNIX system developers was to provide many simple software tools that can be easily combined to produce sophisticated results. To allow UNIX tools to be connected together, they incorporated the following conventions:

1. Output from all tools is written to the **standard output device** (abbreviated *stdout*);

2. Input is read either from the **standard input device** (abbreviated *stdin*) or from a file;

3. Error messages are written to the **standard error device** (abbreviated *stderr*);

4. The shell, not the tool programs, controls the assignment of the standard input, output, and error devices.

The usual standard output device and standard error device is the user's workstation screen. The usual standard input device is the keyboard.

A useful feature of the UNIX system and its shell is that the user can change the assignment of these devices on the shell's command line when a command is entered. This is called standard input/output **redirection**. For example, stdin can be redirected to come from a file, an˙ tdout can be redirected into a file. The individual tool programs still write to stdout and read from stdin—they do not have to be programmed to take advantage of input/output redirection.

Log into your system and set the TERM or term variable if this was required in previous chapters. Recall that in Chapter 4 you created a subdirectory called "launches" to organize your "probes" files. Change the current working directory to that subdirectory by entering the command

```
cd launches
```

Recall the cat command. We saw in the last chapter, during the discussion of file name wildcards, that the cat command syntax permits more than one file, as shown below:

```
cat filenames
```

When given more than one file name, cat will **concatenate** their contents together (one after the other) and output the results to the standard output. To illustrate, enter the command

```
cat probes.50 probes.60 probes.70
```

You should see the contents of these three files displayed on your screen, similar to Fig. 5.1. (Part of the output will scroll off the typical 25-line display screen.)

Recall from Chapter 4 that the UNIX shell permits the use of wildcards for file names. Thus the previous command,

```
cat probes.50 probes.60 probes.70
```

can be abbreviated by using wildcards to

```
cat probes*
```

```
Pioneer 6:Moon:US:65
Surveyor 1:Moon:US:66
Pioneer 7:Sun:US:66
Lunar Orbiter 2:Moon:US:66
Luna 13:Moon:USSR:66
Venera 4:Venus:USSR:67
Surveyor 5:Moon:US:67
Surveyor 6:Moon:US:67
Pioneer 8:Sun:US:67
Pioneer 9:Sun:US:67
Venera 5:Venus:USSR:69
Mariner 6:Mars:US:69
Venera 7:Venus:USSR:70
Luna 17:Moon:USSR:70
Mars 2:Mars:USSR:71
Mariner 9:Mars:US:71
Luna 19:Moon:USSR:71
Pioneer 10:Jupiter:US:72
Venera 8:Venus:USSR:72
Pioneer 11:Jupiter:US:73
Mariner 10:Venus:US:73
Viking 1:Mars:US:75
Voyager 2:Jupiter,Saturn:US:77
Voyager 1:Jupiter,Saturn,Uranus:US:77
$
```

Figure 5.1 Concatenated output from "probes" files (top lines scrolled off).

To store the concatenated output from the cat command, you can redirect the standard output to a file. Enter the command

```
cat probes* > allprobes
```

The > symbol tells the shell to redirect the standard output into the given filename. You can verify this by looking at the contents of the file "allprobes." Enter

```
cat allprobes
```

The output should be identical to Fig. 5.1.

Another UNIX tool is the **wc** (word count) program. The syntax is

```
wc [filename]
```

The wc program counts the number of lines, words, and characters in a file. (The wc command interprets words as groups of characters delimited by either spaces or tabs.)

```
$ wc allprobes
30 61 679
$
```

Figure 5.2   Typical output from the wc command.

Enter the command

    wc allprobes

and you should see output similar to Fig. 5.2. The meaning is 30 lines, 61 words, 679 characters. Thus in all, we have data about 30 space probes in the files "probes.50," "probes.60," and "probes.70."

To make it easy to connect the standard input of one tool into the standard output of another, the UNIX shell provides a mechanism called a **pipe**. Pipes can be used to combine several separate commands into one. For example, to determine that we had data about 30 unmanned space probes in the files "probes*," we followed the steps listed below:

1. Concatenate the probes files together into a single file named allprobes.

2. Use wc to count the number of lines, words, and characters in the allprobes file.

We will use the pipe facility to combine these two operations into one. First, find the ¦ key on your keyboard—it is not the colon, but a key with one or two short vertical bars. Now enter the command

    cat probes* ¦ wc

and you should get the same result counts as shown in Fig. 5.2.

Let us analyze this command. The ¦ character is called a **pipe**. It instructs the shell to take the standard output from the cat command and redirect it into the standard input of the wc command. When the wc command is used without a file name (as above), it looks to the standard input for its input—in this case the standard input is the pipe. Finally, since the output of wc is not redirected, it is displayed on the screen, giving the same results as shown in Fig. 5.2. Figure 5.3 summarizes the shell's redirection symbols.

< *filename*	redirect a file to the standard input
> *filename*	redirect standard output to a file; if the file exists, it is overwritten
>> *filename*	redirect the standard output to a file and append the output to the file
¦	pipe the standard output of one program to the standard input of another

Figure 5.3   Input/output redirection symbols.

UNIX command summary

cat *filenames*	Concatenate files vertically to the standard output
cd	Change directory
wc [*filename*]	Count lines, words, and characters
<	Redirect standard input
>	Redirect standard output
>>	Redirect standard output and append
¦	Pipe standard input to standard output

What Can Go Wrong?

1. When entering a command such as cat probe.50 probes.60 probes.70, a message appears such as

```
cat: cannot open probe.50
```

Cause: The cat program could not find the specified file in the working directory. In this example, "probes.50" was misspelled as "probe.50."

Solution: Check your current directory using the pwd command. If you are not in the "launches" directory, change into it using the cd launches command. Next, enter the ls command and check the names of the files in the "launches" directory. Make sure that you use the names exactly as they appear in the ls command output.

2. The output of the wc program is not the same as shown in Fig. 5.2.

Cause: Your "probes.50," "probes.60," and/or "probes.70" file contains misspelled words or extra lines.

Solution: Use the cat command on each individual file and verify that each file has the correct information. If necessary, use the vi editor to make corrections to your files.

Using UNIX Tools

Sorting

In this section you will use some of the UNIX system tools to manipulate and extract information from your probes files. To begin, consider the abbreviated syntax of the sort command shown in Fig. 5.4.

Using no options, the sort command sorts lines of all the named files together, in ascending order, and sends the result to the standard output. The -r option changes the order of the sort to descending. If no file name is given, sort looks for its input from the standard input. To illustrate, enter the command

```
sort probes.50
```

The output should appear similar to Fig. 5.5.

The options shown in Fig. 5.4 for sort are used when it is necessary to sort the input according to a particular field. The particular field that determines the order of the sort is called the **sort key**. Recall that each line in our "probes" files is made up of four fields delimited by colons, as illustrated below:

```
Lunik 1:Moon:USSR:59
```

The sort command uses a space or tab as its default field delimiter. Since our delimiter is a :, we will use the -t option to specify the field delimiter using the syntax -t:. The options +*pos1* and -*pos2* ("pos" means position) are used to specify which field (or fields) in each line is to be used for the sort key. The option +*pos1* tells how many fields to skip to get to the beginning of the sort key. The option -*pos2* indicates the end of the sort key. For example, to sort by launch destination (e.g., Moon, Mars), we would use the options +1 and -2, since we need to skip one field to get to the destination field (Moon, Mars, etc.), and this sort key ends with the next field.

Try sorting by destination. Enter the command

```
sort -t: +1 -2 probes*
```

You should see output similar to Fig. 5.6 (some output may scroll off the screen).

> **Keystroke and Command Summary: Sorting**
>
> sort [-t*x*] [-r] [+*pos1* [-*pos2*]] [*files*]   sort the given files or
>   the standard input

```
sort [-tx]  [-r]  [+pos1 [-pos2]]  [filenames]
```

Figure 5.4 Abbreviated syntax for the sort command.

```
$ sort probes.50
Lunik 1:Moon:USSR:59
Pioneer 1:Moon:US:58
Pioneer 2:Moon:US:59
$
```

Figure 5.5 Output from the sort command.

What Can Go Wrong?

1. The output from the command: sort -t: +1 -2 probes* is not sorted by destination.

    Cause: You might have a typing error in your sort command.

    Solution: Make sure that you do not have a space in the option -t:. Be sure that there is no space in the filename wildcard probes*. Reenter the command.

```
Mariner 6:Mars:US:69
Mariner 9:Mars:US:71
Mars 2:Mars:USSR:71
Viking 1:Mars:US:75
Luna 13:Moon:USSR:66
Luna 17:Moon:USSR:70
Luna 19:Moon:USSR:71
Lunar Orbiter 2:Moon:US:66
Lunik 1:Moon:USSR:59
Pioneer 1:Moon:US:58
Pioneer 4:Moon:US:59
Pioneer 6:Moon:US:65
Ranger 7:Moon:US:64
Surveyor 1:Moon:US:66
Surveyor 5:Moon:US:67
Surveyor 6:Moon:US:67
Pioneer 7:Sun:US:66
Pioneer 8:Sun:US:67
Pioneer 9:Sun:US:67
Mariner 10:Venus:US:73
Venera 3:Venus:USSR:65
Venera 4:Venus:USSR:67
Venera 5:Venus:USSR:69
Venera 7:Venus:USSR:70
Venera 8:Venus:USSR:72
$
```

Figure 5.6 Sorting by destination (top lines scrolled off).

```
grep pattern [filenames]
```

Figure 5.7 Abbreviated syntax for the grep command.

Searching

Another useful UNIX tool is the **grep** command. This tool searches its input for lines that match a given pattern. The abbreviated syntax is illustrated in Fig. 5.7.

Like wc and sort, grep will accept its input either from a list of files or from the standard input. The *pattern* can be a word or, in the more complex sense, an expression. For this tutorial the pattern will consist of a single word.

To test the grep command, enter the command

```
grep US: probes*
```

The output will consist of all lines containing the characters US:. (Notice that we could not simply grep for US because this would find lines with US and USSR.) The output should resemble Fig. 5.8.

```
$ grep US: probes*
probes.50:Pioneer 1:Moon:US:58
probes.50:Pioneer 4:Moon:US:59
probes.60:Ranger 7:Moon:US:64
probes.60:Mariner 4:Mars:US:64
probes.60:Pioneer 6:Moon:US:65
probes.60:Surveyor 1:Moon:US:66
probes.60:Pioneer 7:Sun:US:66
probes.60:Lunar Orbiter 2:Moon:US:66
probes.60:Surveyor 5:Moon:US:67
probes.60:Surveyor 6:Moon:US:67
probes.60:Pioneer 8:Sun:US:67
probes.60:Pioneer 9:Sun:US:67
probes.60:Mariner 6:Mars:US:69
probes.70:Mariner 9:Mars:US:71
probes.70:Pioneer 10:Jupiter:US:72
probes.70:Pioneer 11:Jupiter:US:73
probes.70:Mariner 10:Venus:US:73
probes.70:Viking 1:Mars:US:75
probes.70:Voyager 2:Jupiter,Saturn:US:77
probes.70:Voyager 1:Jupiter,Saturn,Uranus:US:77
$
```

Figure 5.8 Typical output from the grep command.

You can combine sort and grep into a command that will both sort and search the "probes" files. First, notice the format of one of the lines produced by grep in Fig. 5.8, as illustrated by the line below:

```
probes.50:Pioneer 1:Moon:US:58
```

There is an extra field, the file name, at the start of each line. This new field will have to be taken into account when piping this output to sort. Enter the following command, which will list all US launches sorted by destination:

```
grep US: probes* ¦ sort -t: +2 -3
```

The grep command extracts all lines containing *US:*; this result is piped into sort, which uses the third field of each line from grep as the sort key. The output should resemble Fig. 5.9.

As a further example, to extract all launches to Mars, sort the output by launch year, and store this result in a file called "mars," enter the command

```
grep Mars probes* ¦ sort -t: +4 > mars
```

The output will resemble Fig. 5.10. (The option *-pos2* is not needed above, since the launch year is the last field in the file.) Notice that since the output

```
$ grep US: probes* ¦ sort -t: +2 -3
probes.70:Pioneer 10:Jupiter:US:72
probes.70:Pioneer 11:Jupiter:US:73
probes.70:Voyager 2:Jupiter,Saturn:US:77
probes.70:Voyager 1:Jupiter,Saturn,Uranus:US:77
probes.60:Mariner 4:Mars:US:64
probes.60:Mariner 6:Mars:US:69
probes.70:Mariner 9:Mars:US:71
probes.70:Viking 1:Mars:US:75
probes.50:Pioneer 1:Moon:US:58
probes.50:Pioneer 4:Moon:US:59
probes.60:Lunar Orbiter 2:Moon:US:66
probes.60:Pioneer 6:Moon:US:65
probes.60:Ranger 7:Moon:US:64
probes.60:Surveyor 1:Moon:US:66
probes.60:Surveyor 5:Moon:US:67
probes.60:Surveyor 6:Moon:US:67
probes.60:Pioneer 7:Sun:US:66
probes.60:Pioneer 8:Sun:US:67
probes.60:Pioneer 9:Sun:US:67
probes.70:Mariner 10:Venus:US:73
$
```

Figure 5.9 Typical output from grep piped into sort.

```
$ grep Mars probes* ¦ sort -t: +4 > mars
$
```

Figure 5.10 Redirecting the output into a file.

```
$ grep MARS probes* ¦ wc
      5         10      153
$
```

Figure 5.11 Counting launches to Mars (typical output).

is redirected into the file named "mars," only the UNIX commands are
displayed on the screen.

To determine the number of launches to Mars, enter

    grep Mars probes* ¦ wc

The first line of output from word count (wc) gives the number of lines ex-
tracted by grep. See Fig. 5.11 for a typical response from this command.

> **Keystroke and Command Summary: Searching**
>
> grep *pattern* [*filenames*]   search the input for lines
>   matching the given *pattern*

What Can Go Wrong?

1. The grep command examples do not yield the expected output as
shown in the text.

Cause: You might have a typing mistake in your commands.

Solution: Be sure to enter the commands as shown. Be sure to
use uppercase characters as shown in, for example, US and Mars.

Paginating

Tools such as sort and grep that accept standard input, alter (filter) it in
some way, and then pass it on to the standard output are called **filters**. The
availability of many filters (tools) and the shell's redirection and piping
facilities represent the primary way that the UNIX system provides flexibil-
ity for the user.

UNIX Tools and Utilities   **85**
Using UNIX Tools

Other useful filters are **pr** (print), **more** (on Berkeley systems), and **pg** (on System V). The syntax for these commands is

```
pr [options] [filenames]
more [options] [filenames]
pg [options] [filenames]
```

These commands accept input either from the given file names or from the standard input. Pr divides its input into pages for printing on a hard copy printer, each page having a heading that includes the date and time, page number, and name of the file. More and pg divide their input into pages for viewing on a workstation screen. More is usually found on Berkeley versions of UNIX, while pg is found on some versions of System V. Both more and pg pause after each screenful, display a prompt (– More – for more and : for pg) at the bottom of the screen, and then wait for the user to enter a command. Some commands are the following:

	More commands	Pg commands
Display next page	space bar	⏎
Display next line	⏎	l (ell) *then* ⏎
Help	h	h *then* ⏎
Quit	q	q *then* ⏎

Let's examine these commands.

To produce a paginated listing of the "probes" files, sorted by destination, and to view the output on a workstation screen, enter the command:

```
sort -t: +1 -2 probes* ¦ pr ¦ more
```

The more command will pause after each screen as shown in Fig. 5.12. (If the more command is not found on your system, substitute pg in its place in this and subsequent commands.)

If you are using more, when you see the – More – prompt, press

⏎

and more will display one more line. If you are using pg, at the : prompt, enter

l *then* ⏎

to view the next line of text.

To view the next screenful of data, either press the space bar for more or press ⏎ for pg. Continue using this command until your system completes the file and returns to the shell prompt.

To send the paginated listing to the system printer instead of to the screen, pipe the output from pr into lpr (or lp) instead of more. The following command will sort the contents of the "probes" files (sorted on the second field),

```
Jul 15 12:57 1989 Page 1

Pioneer 10:Jupiter:US:72
Pioneer 11:Jupiter:US:73
Voyager 2:Jupiter,Saturn:US:77
Voyager 1:Jupiter,Saturn,Uranus:US:77
Mariner 4:Mars:US:64
Mariner 6:Mars:US:69
Mariner 9:Mars:US:71
Mars 2:Mars:USSR:71
Viking 1:Mars:US:75
Luna 13:Moon:USSR:66
Luna 17:Moon:USSR:70
Luna 19:Moon:USSR:71
Lunar Orbiter 2:Moon:US:66
Lunik 1:Moon:USSR:59
Pioneer 1:Moon:US:58
Pioneer 4:Moon:US:59
Pioneer 6:Moon:US:65
— More —
```

Figure 5.12 Typical output from more.

paginate the sorted output, and send the paginated output to the system printer:

```
sort -t: +1 -2 probes* ¦ pr ¦ lpr
```

Like pr and more, both lpr and lp will accept their input either from a file or from the standard input. (*Note:* If you enter this command, substitute your print command for lpr.)

> ### Keystroke and Command Summary: Paginating
>
> | | |
> |---|---|
> | lpr [*filenames*] | send the given input to the system printer (Berkeley) |
> | lp [*filenames*] | send the given input to the system printer (System V) |
> | more [*options*] [*filenames*] | paginate input for visual displays (Berkeley) |
> | pg [*options*] [*filenames*] | paginate input for visual displays (System V) |
> | pr [*options*] [*filenames*] | paginate input for hard copy output |

What Can Go Wrong?

1. When attempting to use the more command, the system responds

```
more: not found
```

Cause: Your system does not have the more command.

Solution 1: Use pg in place of more. If this fails, see Solution 2.

Solution 2: You can pause the screen by pressing Ctrl *and* s while data is being displayed on your screen. To resume the output, press Ctrl *and* q.

Getting Help

The On-line Manual Pages

The UNIX system has hundreds of tool and utility programs. They are documented in the UNIX reference manuals, which are both printed and available on line on most UNIX systems. For each tool, an entry in the reference manual presents a description, the valid options, and some simple examples.

To view an on-line manual page for a command, you will use the **man** (manual) command. On some systems the man command will pause after each screenful of data. If your system pauses, press the space bar to move to the next screen. Enter the following:

```
man sort
```

The abbreviated output from this command is shown in Fig. 5.13.

Some smaller UNIX systems do not support the on-line manual pages. If you received the message

```
man: not found
```

you will have to use your organization's printed manual pages. However, you should still read this section, since it explains how to read both the printed and on-line manual pages.

If the output of the man command did not pause between screens, you will have to pipe the output of the man command into the more or pg filter. For example, you would enter

```
man sort ¦ pg
```

and then press ↵ to view each screenful of data. If your system does not have more or pg, then use Ctrl *and* s and Ctrl *and* q to control scrolling.

```
SORT(1)                                              SORT(1)

NAME
     sort - sort and/or merge files

SYNOPSIS
     sort [-cmu] [-ooutput] -ykmem] [-rrecsz] [-dfiMnr] [-btx]
     [+pos1 [-pos2]] [files]

DESCRIPTION
     Sort sorts lines of all the named files together and writes
     the result on the standard output. The standard input is
     read if - is used as a file name or no input files are
     named.
     ...

OPTIONS
     C    Check that the input file is sorted according to the
          ordering rules; give no output unless the file is out
          of sort.
     ...

EXAMPLES
     Sort the contents of infile with the second filed as the
     sort key:
             sort +1 -2 infile
     ...

SEE ALSO
     comm(1), join(1), uniq(1).

DIAGNOSTICS
     Comments and exits with nonzero status for various trouble
     conditions ...

RESTRICTIONS
     Sort output files without truncation if the file has up to
     46,380 lines ...

SUPPORT STATUS
     Supported.
```

Figure 5.13   Example of man command output.

Examine the categories of information in Fig. 5.13. These are explained in
Fig. 5.14.

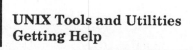

UNIX Tools and Utilities
Getting Help

```
COMMAND-NAME(manual section number)
     The UNIX manual is divided into 8 sections, numbered 1
     through 8. The section number is given in parentheses, and
     corresponds to the following topics:
     Section      Topic
     1            Commands available to users
     2            UNIX and C system calls
     3            C library routines for C programs
     4            Special file names
     5            File formats and conventions (files used by
                  UNIX)
     6            Games
     7            Word processing packages
     8            System administrator commands and procedures

NAME
     Brief description of the tool

SYNOPSIS
     Syntax for the tool

DESCRIPTION
     Detailed description

OPTIONS
     Explanation of each option

EXAMPLES

SEE ALSO
     The names of related commands

DIAGNOSTICS
     Error messages and brief descriptions

SUPPORT STATUS
     Categories are: supported and unsupported.
```

Figure 5.14 Format of a UNIX manual page.

For tools that have long manual pages, you might want to locate your organization's printed manuals. Alternatively, you can print a copy of the on-line manual pages. To do so, pipe the output of the man command into the lpr (or lp) command. You should avoid generating excessive printed output so that the printer is not tied up.

```
bsearch(3)              - binary search a sorted table
comm(1)                 - compare sorted data
look(1)                 - find lines in sorted data
qsort(3)                - quick sort
qsort(3f)               - quicker FORTRAN sort
sort(1)                 - sort file data
sortbib(1)              - sort bibliographic database
sortm(1)                - sort messages
tsort(1)                - create topological sort
```

Figure 5.15 Output from the apropos command.

Finding Commands about a Topic

Many UNIX systems, especially those based on the Berkeley version, provide the **apropos** command ("apropos" means "relating to"). Apropos does a keyword search of the on-line manual pages and displays command names, manual section, and a brief description of each command that relates to a given keyword. Suppose, for example, that you need to find a UNIX command to work with sorted information. Enter the following command to locate commands that use or produce sorted data:

        apropos sort

The output is illustrated in Fig. 5.15.
    If you received the message

        apropos: not found

try entering the command

        help sort

If you receive the message

        help: not found

then your system does not support these commands. Your alternative is to use the table of contents and the permuted index that is found in the printed UNIX manuals. The permuted index is organized by topic.

Error Messages from Incomplete Commands

Certain UNIX commands require arguments, such as file names, that tell the command an object with which to work. For example, the grep command

        grep US: probes.60

has two arguments: the pattern *US:* and the file name *probes.60*. Commands that require arguments will give you a short diagnostic message if you enter an incomplete command. For example, enter

```
grep
```

On some UNIX systems, you will see a message similar to the following:

```
usage: grep [-blcnsvi] pattern [files]
```

This message is telling you the various options for grep and its requirement for the pattern and optional file name. Some UNIX commands output the message

```
arg count
```

to indicate that the proper number of arguments (e.g., file names) have not been specified.

> **Keystroke and Command Summary: Getting help**
> UNIX command summary:
>
> man *command*   to get help about a *command*
>
> apropos *topic*   to find commands that relate to a *topic*
> or
> help *topic*

What Can Go Wrong?

1. When you use the man command, the output scrolls off the screen too quickly for you to read it.

Cause: The output from the man command on your system is not piped into more or pg.

Solution 1: Pipe the man command into more. For example, enter

```
man sort ¦ more
```

and use the space bar or ⏎ or man sort I pg to move between screens.

Solution 2: You can stop and resume output by using the XON/XOFF (transmit on/off) keystrokes. Press

Ctrl *and* s

to stop the output. Press

Ctrl *and* q

to resume the output.

2. When you enter man sort or apropos sort, the system responds with

```
man: not found
```

or

```
apropos: not found
```

Cause: The man and/or apropos command is not supported on your system.

Solution: If the on-line manuals are not supported on your system, you will have to use the printed documentation. The UNIX system documentation provides a permuted index by topic to help you find commands based on a keyword (such as apropos). Otherwise, the documentation is organized into sections, each containing manual pages about UNIX system commands. You will use Section 1, "Commands Available to Users."

This concludes Chapter 5. At this time you should log off of your UNIX account and complete the self-test at the end of this chapter.

Command Summary

apropos *topic*	display names of commands related to a specific topic
cat *filenames*	concatenate the specified filenames and send the output to the standard output
cd *directory*	change current directory
help *topic*	another name for apropos on some systems
lpr [*filenames*]	print the specified files or the standard input (Berkeley)
lp [*filenames*]	print the specified files or the standard input (System V)
man *command*	display on-line manual pages for command
more [*filenames*]	paginate input for visual displays
pg [*filenames*]	paginate input for visual displays

pr [*filenames*]	paginate the contents of the specified files or the standard input for printing
grep *pattern* [*filenames*]	search for lines with the given pattern
sort [-*tx*] [+*pos1* [-*pos2*]] [*filenames*]	sort specified files or standard input
wc [*filename*]	count words, lines, and characters
<	redirect standard input from a file
>	redirect standard output to a file
>>	redirect standard output and append to a file
¦	pipe the standard output into standard input

Self-Test

program or command

1. UNIX tools follow a convention of writing their output to the _____ and reading their input from the _____.

2. A tool that accepts input and passes it on as output in a modified form is called a _____.

3. In the blanks below, specify the appropriate shell redirection *symbol* to perform the desired functions:

   a. ___ redirects the output of a tool into the input of another tool.

   b. ___ redirects the output of a tool into a file, overwriting the file if it exists.

   c. ___ redirects the output of a tool into a file but appends the output to the file.

   d. ___ redirects the contents of a file into the standard input of a tool

4. The command to search for UNIX commands based on a keyword is _____.

   apropos

5. Compose a command that will print (on the printer) the manual page for the grep command: _man grep | lpr_   *man grep | lpr*

6. Modify the command in Question 5 so that the on-line manual page for grep is *paginated for hard copy* output but still displayed on the workstation screen:

   _____

7. Compose a command that will display all lines in the files "probes.50," "probes.60," and "probes.70" that were launched by the USSR: _____

   cat probes.[5-7]0 | more

94

8. Modify the command in Question 7 to give the number of probes launched by the USSR: _____

9. Compose a command that will display all the lines in the files "probes.50," "probes.60," and "probes.70" that include the word "Venus," such that the output is sorted by country. The sort command will require the options -t, +pos1, and -pos2. Remember that +pos1 and -pos2 tell the sort command which field(s) to use for the sort key. _____

10. Modify the command in Question 9 by using input/output redirection such that the output from the command is stored in a file named "venus" _____

11. Compose a command that will display all of the lines in the files "probes.50," "probes.60," and "probes.70," concatenated together, on the workstation screen such that the output pauses after each screenful of data so that you can view the data without it scrolling off the display: _____

Exercises

1. List two ways to get help regarding a UNIX command.

2. If you completed Exercise 2 or Exercise 3 in Chapter 3, then you have a telephone directory file. Use the UNIX sort command to sort that file by name. Then sort it by phone number. Finally, resort it by name and redirect the output from that command into a file named phone.sort.

3. Use the wc command to determine the number of lines and characters in your telephone directory file.

4. Use the grep command to search your file for a particular name. Then use grep to search the file for a particular phone number or street address.

5. Sort your telephone directory file by name, but pipe the output into the pr filter. Repeat this command again, but this time, pipe the output of pr to your printer.

grep USSR probes.50 — — | wc
grep Venus probes.50 ; ; | sort >

6

Customizing Your UNIX Account

This chapter:

- describes the protection mode for files and how to use permissions for files

- describes the protection mode for directories and how to use permissions for directories

- illustrates the use of the .profile or .login files

- introduces the C shell initialization file .cshrc

- introduces ways to customize how UNIX works

At this point in the tutorial you know that the UNIX system provides a file system composed of directories that are organized in hierarchical fashion. The top-level directory is called the root and is designated by the / symbol. Under the root are files and subdirectories. Each user who has a UNIX system account will have a private subdirectory within the file system to hold his or her files. This chapter will further investigate the file system and will present ways in which you can customize and control your UNIX account.

File and Directory Permissions

Examining and Changing File Permissions

Multiuser systems such as the UNIX operating system must provide security measures to ensure the integrity and privacy of the system as a whole and of all user files in particular. One security measure that guards the system as a whole is the requirement of a password at the time that you log into the UNIX system. Another security measure is file permissions. To protect the privacy of user information, each file and directory has associated with it a set of **permissions** that determine whether the file can be read, written, or executed by various classes of users. The UNIX system allows you to set the permissions for your own directories and files. Let's look at file permissions.

Log into your UNIX system and set your terminal type if this was required earlier. To view the permissions for all of the files in your current directory, enter the following ls command, with the long (-l) and all (-a) options:

    ls -la

The output should resemble Fig. 6.1a (System V) or Fig. 6.1b (Berkeley).

```
$ls -la
total 4
drwxrwxrwx   3    troyd      64    May 30   15:20  .
drwxrwxrwx   6    troyd     608    May 30   15:06  ..
-rwxrwxrwx   1    troyd      11    Mar  2    9:08  .profile
drwxrwxrwx   2    troyd     128    May 30   15:21  launches
$
```

Figure 6.1(a)   Typical output of ls -la (System V).

```
%ls -la
total 8
drwxrwxrwx   3    troyd      64    May 30   15:20  .
drwxrwxrwx   6    troyd     608    May 30   15:06  ..
-rwxrwxrwx   1    troyd      41    Mar  2    9:10  .cshrc
-rwxrw-rw-   1    troyd     588    May 30   15:22  .history
-rwxrwxrwx   1    troyd      98    Mar  2    9:10  .login
drwxrwxrwx   2    troyd      24    Mar  2    9:10  bin
drwxrwxrwx   2    troyd     128    May 30   15:21  launches
%
```

Figure 6.1(b)   Typical output of ls -la (Berkeley).

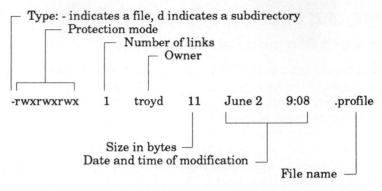

Figure 6.2 Information about files.

The -l option causes ls to present one line of information for each file in the current working directory. The listing from your directory may vary somewhat according to the way in which your UNIX system has been configured. Also, you might not have some of the files that start with a "dot" such as .profile, .login, or .cshrc; these are used to customize your UNIX account and will be discussed later in this chapter. For the moment, let us consider the general meaning of one of the lines in Fig. 6.1.

Figure 6.2 presents the meaning of each entry in the long listing. The listing shows that the file named .profile was last modified (with an editor) on June 2 at 9:08, the file contains 11 bytes (or characters) of information, it is owned by user troyd, and it has one link. The owner of a file is assigned when the file is created. Links permit a particular file to have more than one name; this file has only one link. The string "rwxrwxrwx" gives the protection mode string, which is used to indicate permissions for the file. Permissions are explained below. The leftmost character is the type of entry: a dash indicates an ordinary file, d indicates a subdirectory.

Notice the other files listed in Fig. 6.1. The first file is named "dot" (.). This is a shorthand name for the current working directory. The file named "dot-dot" (..) is a synonym for this directory's parent directory. These two files are created automatically by the UNIX system when a directory is created. The entry "launches" is the name of the subdirectory that you created in an earlier tutorial to hold your "probes" files.

Now enter the command

    ls

The corresponding output from the UNIX System V machine that generated the output in Fig. 6.1a is illustrated in Fig. 6.3. Notice that the file names that begin with a dot are not listed in Fig. 6.3. File names that start with a dot are not displayed unless the -a (all) option is used with ls because these files are used only occasionally by the user.

```
$ ls
launches
$
```

Figure 6.3 Output of ls for the same directory as Fig. 6.1a.

The permissions for a file are indicated by the **protection mode string**. The protection mode string for the file .profile from Fig. 6.2 is explained in Fig. 6.4.

Notice that there are three categories of users for whom you may give permissions for your file: the **owner** (yourself), **group**, and **others**. The owner and group are assigned to a file when it is created. When you create a file, you become the owner. You are also in a group, which is assigned by the system administrator when your account was generated. Generally, all users are in the same group, so for this text we will not need to discuss the concept of groups. A user who is not the owner and not in the same group as the owner falls into the category of other.

For each category of users you can assign three different permissions: read (r), write (w), and execute (x). The presence of the r, w, or x character in the protection mode string indicates that the respective permission is granted. A dash in place of one of these three characters indicates that the corresponding permission is denied. Let's examine how permissions might be used.

Change the current working directory to the "launches" subdirectory by entering the command cd launches and then enter the command ls -l. The sequence of commands that you should enter and the associated output is illustrated in Fig. 6.5. Notice that the "dot" and "dot-dot" directory names are not shown because we did not include the -a option in the ls command.

Examine the protection mode strings in Fig. 6.5 and compare them to your output. In Fig. 6.5, each file has read (r) and write (w) permissions given for all three user categories but no execute (x) permissions. An executable file is

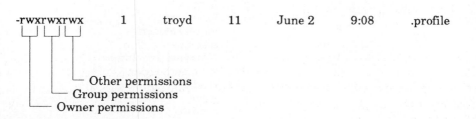

Figure 6.4 Protection mode string.

```
$ cd launches
$ ls -l
total 5
-rw-rw-rw   1    troyd    680   May 30   15:11   allprobes
-rw-rw-rw   1    troyd    153   May 31   09:16   mars
-rw-rw-rw   1    troyd     63   May 16   11:30   probes.50
-rw-rw-rw   1    troyd    326   May 16   15:12   probes.60
-rw-rw-rw   1    troyd    291   May 20   12:22   probes.70
$
```

Figure 6.5 Typical long directory listing of "launches" subdirectory.

one that holds a program. None of the files in the "launches" subdirectory are programs.

Now suppose that the "allprobes" file contains confidential information. You might therefore want to make this file unreadable by anyone but yourself. To do this, you will need to change that file's permissions, using the UNIX command **chmod** (change mode). The syntax for chmod is shown in Fig. 6.6.

The letters for the *who* argument represent categories of users. These letters may be combined to indicate more than one category. Similarly, the permissions may be combined to represent multiple permissions. Let's remove read and write permissions for the group and other categories from the "allprobes" file. Enter the command

```
chmod go-rw allprobes
```

chmod *who op permission filenames*

where:
who	u	for owner
	g	for group
	o	for others
	a	for all categories
op	+	add a permission
	-	remove a permission
	=	set a permission
permission	r	read
	w	write
	x	execute

Figure 6.6 Syntax for chmod.

```
$ chmod go-rw allprobes
$ ls -l allprobes
-rw------      1      troyd    680    May 30    15:12 allprobes
$
```

Figure 6.7 New protection mode for the `allprobes` file.

The argument *go* means "group, others"; the argument - means to remove; and the argument *rw* means "read, write". Now enter the command

> ls -l allprobes

The output should be as shown in Fig. 6.7.

Now the only permissions for this file are read/write for the owner. This means that only the owner may view or change the file. (Actually, the system administrator, called the **super-user**, can read and write any file. If you can't trust your super-user, whom can you trust?)

For the sake of illustration, try removing read the owner's permissions from the "allprobes" file, and then try to display its contents using the cat command. Enter the commands shown in Fig. 6.8, and you should see the output similar to that shown in that figure.

Notice that after you removed the read permission, the UNIX system would not allow you to read the contents of the file. The message cannot open allprobes means that that file could not be "opened" for reading. Be sure to restore read access to the file by using the last chmod command shown in Fig. 6.8.

> **Keystroke and Command Summary: Examining and changing file permissions**
>
> UNIX command summary
>
> | | |
> |---|---|
> | cat *filename* | display a file's contents |
> | cd *subdirectory* | make subdirectory be the current working directory |
> | chmod *who op permission file* | change a file's permissions |

```
$ chmod u-r allprobes
$ cat allprobes
cat: cannot open allprobes
$ chmod u+r allprobes
$
```

Figure 6.8 Attempting to access a protected file (typical output).

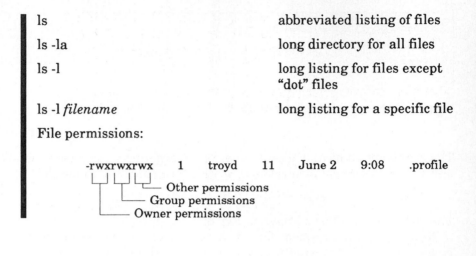

ls	abbreviated listing of files
ls -la	long directory for all files
ls -l	long listing for files except "dot" files
ls -l *filename*	long listing for a specific file

File permissions:

-rwxrwxrwx   1   troyd   11   June 2   9:08   .profile

     — Other permissions
    — Group permissions
   — Owner permissions

What Can Go Wrong?

1. When you issue the ls -la command, you do not find any of the files shown in the tutorial.

 Cause: You are probably not in the correct directory.

 Solution: Enter the pwd command to determine your current working directory. Change to the proper directory using cd and retry the command.

2. When you issue the ls -la command, you see most of the files in the tutorial, but some of the information differs from that shown in the figures.

 Cause: Information such as the creation date will correspond to the date and time that you last edited (or first created) your files. The number of bytes may differ if you have entered different words into your files. The permissions may vary. There may be additional or fewer files listed.

 Solution: These are not problems. UNIX systems vary in the files that are installed into new accounts and the default permissions that are assigned to new files.

3. When you use the chmod command, the following message appears

```
chmod: cannot access filename
```

 Cause: The name of the file or directory whose mode you are trying to change is misspelled, or you are in the wrong directory.

Solution: Verify the correct spelling of the file name. If it is correct, use the pwd command to verify your current working directory and then use the cd command if necessary to change to the proper directory.

4. When you use the chmod command, the following message appears

```
chmod: invalid mode
```

Cause: The permission part of the command is entered incorrectly. The permissions discussed in this section are rwx.

Solution: Double-check the way in which you entered the command. See Fig. 6.6 for the proper syntax of the command.

Permissions for Directories

The meanings of the read, write, and execute permissions for directories are different from the meanings for files. The meanings for directories are given in Figure 6.9.

Some UNIX utility programs directly read the directory (to get information about files) as if it is a file. The read permission must be set for a directory to permit this operation. The write permission allows a category of users to create and remove files in a directory. The execute permission allows access to a directory so that files in it can be read.

If you are following along with this tutorial, your current directory should be "launches." You can verify this by entering the pwd command. Now suppose that you want to keep prying eyes out of *all* of the files in the "launches" subdirectory. To do this, enter the command

```
chmod go-x .
```

This command removes read permission for the group and other categories of users for the current ("dot") directory. Now verify the protection mode for the current directory by entering the following ls command using the -l and -d (directory) options:

```
ls -ld .
```

Your screen should resemble Fig. 6.10.

r   Allow utility programs to read the directory as if it is a file.
w   Permit creation and removal of files in the directory.
x   Permit access to the files in the directory. This allows files to be displayed, copied, etc.

Figure 6.9   Permissions for directories.

```
$ pwd
/usr/acct/troyd/launches
$ chmod go-x .
$ls -ld .
drwxrw-rw-    2 troyd       144   May 30  15:14   .
$
```

Figure 6.10   Changing permissions for a directory (typical display from the author's system).

Let us verify the protection mode for the "launches" subdirectory by viewing the protection mode from your home directory. One way to change the current directory from "launches" to the home directory is to enter the command **cd ..**, since "launches" is a subdirectory of your home directory. Another way to set the working directory to your home directory, no matter what its current setting, is simply to enter the cd command with no arguments. Do this now. Enter

> cd

Now verify the protection mode for the "launches" subdirectory by entering:

> ls -ld launches

You should see the identical protection mode as shown in Fig. 6.10. *Note:* If you enter ls -1 launches, UNIX will display a listing of the files in the "launches" subdirectory; the -d option is required in order to view the protection mode for the directory itself.

You can protect *all* of your personal files and directories by removing the x permission from your home directory. Enter

> chmod go-x .

to remove read access permissions for both group and other users for your home directory. This is a good idea, since users are free to roam the UNIX file system, prying and peeking, to see what there is to see on the system.

> **Keystroke and Command Summary: Permissions for directories**
> UNIX command summary
>
> | | |
> |---|---|
> | cd | change the current working directory to the home directory |
> | cd .. | change the current working directory to the parent |
> | chmod *who op permission directory* | change a directory's permissions |

ls -ld *directory*   list information about a directory

ls -l *directory*   list information about the files in a directory

pwd   print current working directory

Directory permissions

r   The directory may be read as if it is a file.

w   Entries in the directory may be created and removed.

x   Access to the files and directories in this directory is permitted.

What Can Go Wrong?

1. When you use the chmod command, the following message appears:

```
Usage: chmod [ugoa] [+-=] [rwxstugo] file...
```

Cause: Your chmod command is missing an argument or has an incorrect argument. The syntax is

```
chmod who op permissions file
```

Remember, for some of the commands in this section the file name was simply "dot" for the current directory.

Solution: See Fig. 6.6 for the syntax, and be sure to enter the command as shown in the text. You can get additional help from your UNIX reference manuals and by using the command man chmod.

Customizing Your UNIX Account

Login Command Files

The UNIX system has been designed to work with various kinds of computers and workstations. For example, we noted that the UNIX shells have the variables TERM (Bourne shell) and term (C shell) that hold the name of the terminal (workstation) to which UNIX thinks you are connected. We also used the stty command to view the setting of the kill and erase characters, which can also be changed to suit a particular user. These kinds of UNIX commands are used to configure the UNIX system properly to your hardware and taste. Configuration commands that must be entered each time you log in can be put into a "login command file" for the shell to read and execute automatically each time that you log in.

```
Bourne shell:    .profile
C shell:         .login
```

Figure 6.11   Login command file names.

The name of the login command file depends on the shell in use. For the Bourne shell and C shell the names are shown in Fig. 6.11.

If you need to set your terminal type each time you log in, you should edit (or create) your login command file using the vi editor and enter the command to set the terminal type into that file. Figure 6.12a shows a typical example of a Bourne shell .profile file, and Fig. 6.12b presents an example of a C shell .login file.

You can see that the purpose of most of the commands in Figs. 6.12a and 6.12b is to give values to shell variables. Some important shell variables that are used by UNIX and some of its programs are listed in Fig. 6.13.

One variable from Fig. 6.13 that is worth noting is the PATH (or path) variable. On the UNIX system, most commands are carried out by having the shell execute a program. When you enter a command like cat, sort, or vi, the shell searches certain directories for a file with the corresponding name and then executes that file. Most of the UNIX commands are stored in the "/bin" and "/usr/bin" directories. The PATH (or path) environment variable gives the shell the list of directories to be searched whenever a command is entered.

```
TERM=vt100
export TERM
PATH=.:/usr/ucb:/bin:/usr/bin:/usr/local
MAIL=/usr/spool/mail/$USER
PS1="$"
stty echoe
date
who
```

Figure 6.12(a)   Example of a typical Bourne shell .profile file.


```
set TERM=vt100
setenv MAIL /usr/spool/mail/$USER
set mail=$MAIL
set path=(. /usr/ucb /bin /usr/bin /usr/local)
set prompt="%"
stty echoe
date
who
```

Figure 6.12(b)   Example of a typical C shell .login file

Shell variable		*Purpose*
Bourne	*C shell*	
TERM	term	the name of the users terminal type
MAIL	mail	the file pathname for the users E-mail mailbox
PATH	path	a list of directories that are to be searched by the shell whenever a command is entered by the user
PS1	prompt	the prompt string to be displayed by the shell

UNIX commands

stty echoe	cause the shell to remove characters from the screen as they are erased
date	display the system date and time
who	display a list of logged on users

Figure 6.13 Some typical login command file variables and commands.

This list of directories is called the **search path**. You will notice that the first directory in the search paths shown in Figs. 6.12a and 6.12b is the "dot" directory. This means that the shell first looks for files in your current working directory and then searches the other directories in the search path. Thus to add a new command to UNIX, a user need only create the program, store it in one of the directories in the search path, and then enter the program's file name at the shell prompt.

C Shell Command File

In addition to executing commands from the .login file at login time, the C shell executes commands in the .cshrc file each time a shell is started. The difference between the .cshrc and .login files is that the commands in .login are executed only if the shell is the user's "login" shell. The commands in .cshrc are executed if the shell is the login shell and also if it is another instance of the C shell. Sophisticated UNIX users sometimes start up additional instances of the shell after logging in. These additional instances will execute the commands in .cshrc but not in .login. (*Note:* The name .cshrc is read "C shell rc." By convention, *rc* is used in a file name to indicate a file of commands to be read by a program when it starts.)

At logoff time the C shell will execute commands in the file .logout.

Using the Ideas

Let's try using some of the shell variables that are shown in Fig. 6.12. To begin, enter the command

        set

You will see output similar to that shown in Fig. 6.14a (Bourne shell) or Fig. 6.14b (C shell).

The **set** command displays the value of all shell variables in your environment. It will also remind you of which of the two shells you are using, since the output of the set command is quite different in appearance for the two shells.

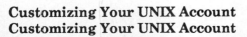

```
$ set
HOME=/usr/acct/troyd
IFS=

LOGNAME=troyd
MAIL=/usr/spool/mail/troyd
MAILCHECK=600
PATH=.:/usr/ucb:/bin:/usr/bin:/usr/local
PS1=$
PS2=>
SHELL=/bin/sh
TERM=vt100
TZ=US/Eastern
$
```

Figure 6.14(a)   Output from the set command for Bourne shell.

```
% set
argv    ()
cwd     /usr/acct/troyd
history 20
home    /usr/acct/troyd
mail    /usr/spool/mail/troyd
notify
path    (. /usr/ucb /bin /usr/bin /usr/local)
prompt  %
shell   /bin/csh
status  0
term    vt100
user    troyd
%
```

Figure 6.14(b)   Output from the set command for C shell.

To examine the values of individual shell variables, you can use the **echo** command. Enter the left-hand command if you are using the Bourne shell; enter the right-hand command if you are using the C shell:

      echo $PATH   **or**   echo $path

Echo displays the value of each of its arguments. In this case the argument is the *value* of the shell variable PATH (or path). This is indicated by the presence of the $ sign before the shell variable name.

```
$ set prompt="yes? "
yes?
```

Figure 6.15   Changing the prompt for the C shell.

Now change your shell prompt. Enter the left-hand command for the Bourne shell; enter the right-hand command for the C shell:

PS1="yes? "   or   set prompt="yes? "

Your system should now prompt with the question *yes?* as illustrated in Fig. 6.15. (*Note:* Figure 6.15 shows the C shell command to change the prompt.)

You might now want to create (or edit) your login command file. C shell users will use the file .login, while Bourne shell users will use .profile. You can put in the command to set your terminal type, you can modify your prompt character, and you can add commands such as date and who if you would like to see this information each time that you log into the system.

Keyword and Command Summary: Customizing your UNIX account

Login command files

.login   for the C shell

.profile   for the Bourne shell

Other C shell command files

.cshrc

.logout

UNIX commands

date	remove characters from the screen
echo $*variable*	display the value of a shell variable
set	view shell variables
stty echoe	remove erased characters from the screen
who	display who is logged in

Important shell variables (Bourne shell, C shell)

PATH, path	the directory search path
PS1, prompt	the shell prompt

What Can Go Wrong?

1. After you enter `echo $path` or `echo $PATH`, the system responds with the output `path` or `PATH`.

Cause: Either you forgot to include the dollar sign, you followed it with a space, or the path (or PATH) variable is not defined.

Solution: Be sure to enter the $ sign followed immediately by the word path or PATH. Don't include a space after the $ sign, but do separate the word echo from the $ with a space.

2. After you enter `PS1="yes?"` or `set prompt="yes?"`, the prompt does not change.

Cause: You cannot precede or follow the equal sign in the command with a space.

Solution: Be sure to enter the command exactly as shown, without spaces.

3. After you enter the command `PS1="yes? "`, the system responds

```
PS1=yes? : Command not found
```

Cause: You entered a Bourne shell command, and you are using the C shell.

Solution: Use the command `set prompt="yes?"`

4. After you enter the command `set prompt="yes?"` the prompt character does not change.

Cause: You entered a C shell command, and you are using the Bourne shell.

Solution: Use the command `PS1="yes?"`.

At this time you should log out of your UNIX system and review your understanding of this chapter by completing the end-of-chapter self-test.

| Command Summary

UNIX Commands

cat *filename*	display the contents of a file
cd	change the current directory to your home
cd ..	change the current directory to the parent directory

date	display the date and time
echo $*variable*	display the value of a shell variable
chmod *who op permission file*	change permissions for a file or directory
ls	abbreviated list of files
ls -l	long directory listing of files except "dot" files
ls -la	long directory listing including "dot" files
ls -l *filename*	long directory listing for a single file
ls -ld *directory*	list information about a directory itself
ls -l *directory*	list the contents of a directory
PS1=*value*	change the prompt for the Bourne shell
set	list shell variables and their values
set prompt=*value*	change the prompt for the C shell
stty echoe	remove erased characters from the screen
who	display who is logged in

File and Directory Protection Mode and Permissions

```
-rwxrwxrwx    1    troyd    11    June 2    9:08    .profile
 |_||_||_|
   |  |  |_____ Other permissions
   |  |_____ Group permissions
   |_____ Owner permissions
```

For files:

r = read, w = write, x = execute

For directories:

r = read the directory

w = create and remove entries in the directory

x = permit access to the files and directories in the directory

Self-Test

1. State the UNIX command to perform each of the following operations:

   a. List the names of all of the files in a directory and view the protection mode for each file.

   b. From your home directory, list the protection mode for the "launches" subdirectory.

   c. Change the protection mode for your current directory to deny access to any of the files by others.

   d. Add execute permissions to the file "myfile" for owner and group.

   e. From the current directory, no matter what it may be, change the current directory to your home directory.

   f. From the current directory, change to its parent directory.

   g. Change the prompt for your version of UNIX to -->.

2. Consider the following directory entry:

   -rwxr-x---   1   root   32567   Feb 5   1988   cfit

   Answer the following questions about this entry.

   a. State the permissions for the owner.

   b. State the permissions for others.

   c. State the size of the file.

   d. State the owner of the file.

   e. State the name of the file.

   f. Is the file a directory?

3. For your shell, state the name of the login command file.

4. The file name "dot" is a synonym for _____.

5. To display the value of the shell variable TERM, enter the command _____.

6. The name for the list of paths that are searched whenever a command is entered is called the _____.

Exercises

1. For this exercise you will use the telephone directory file and the phone subdirectory that you created in previous chapter exercises. Give the command that will perform the following operations.

   a. Remove read, write, and execute permissions from the telephone directory file for the group and other categories of users.

   b. Remove access to files in the phone subdirectory for the group and other categories of users.

2. Determine if your UNIX account has a login command file. If it does, answer the following questions about the contents of that file.

   a. Does your login command file specify a search path? If so, give the search path.

   b. Does the command file specify a value for the terminal type? If so, give the terminal type.

3. Enter the set command on your system. Answer the following questions by viewing the output of the set command.

   a. Give your search path.

   b. Give the complete pathname for your shell.

   c. Give your terminal type.

7

Advanced
vi Editing

This chapter:

- describes how to page through text

- describes how to search through text

- describes some convenient shortcut commands

- describes how to copy and move lines in a file

- describes commands for changing multiple lines in a file

- describes how to read and write one file into another

- describes how to recover an editing session after a crash

Chapters 2 and 3 described the use of the vi editor for creating and editing text files. Figure 7.1 summarizes the vi commands that you used in those two chapters. This chapter will present additional vi commands that will allow you to work with longer files and to work more effectively.

At this time you should go to your workstation and log into your UNIX system. Change the current working directory to the "launches" subdirectory by entering

```
cd launches
```

(Esc)	leave insert mode, return to command mode
a	enter insert mode after the cursor
j	move cursor down one line
k	move cursor up one line
h	move cursor left one character
l	move cursor right one character
dd	delete a line
i	enter insert mode before the cursor
O	insert a line above the cursor
o	insert a line below the cursor
r	replace a character
u	undo previous command
x	delete a character
:	go to the command line
:wq	write the file and quit
:q!	exit vi without writing the file

Figure 7.1 Review of vi commands.

```
$ cd launches
$ ls
allprobes    mars    probes.50    probes.60    probes.70
$
```

Figure 7.2 Files in the "launches" subdirectory.

Now enter the command

    ls

You should see the files listed in Fig. 7.2 in your directory. If you do not have the file named "allprobes," you can recreate it by entering

    cat probes* > allprobes

Moving through the File

The "allprobes" file contains 30 lines of text. Bring this file into vi by entering

    vi allprobes

Your screen should now resemble Fig. 7.3

```
Pioneer 1:Moon:US:58
Pioneer 4:Moon:US:59
Lunik 1:Moon:USSR:59
Ranger 7:Moon:US:64
Mariner 4:Mars:US:64
Venera 3:Venus:USSR:65
Pioneer 6:Moon:US:65
Surveyor 1:Moon:US:66
Pioneer 7:Sun:US:66
Lunar Orbiter 2:Moon:US:66
Luna 13:Moon:USSR:66
Venera 4:Venus:USSR:67
Surveyor 5:Moon:US:67
Surveyor 6:Moon:US:67
Pioneer 8:Sun:US:67
Pioneer 9:Sun:US:67
Venera 5:Venus:USSR:69
Mariner 6:Mars:US:69
Venera 7:Venus:USSR:70
Luna 17:Moon:USSR:70
Mars 2:Mars:USSR:71
Mariner 9:Mars:US:71
Luna 19:Moon:USSR:71
"allprobes" 30 lines, 679 characters
```

Figure 7.3   The allprobes file in vi (typical display).

Notice that on all except very large screens, all 30 lines cannot be displayed. vi gives you a window into a large file. In Fig. 7.3 the window displays
23 lines. To move the window through the file, use the vi commands shown in
Fig. 7.4.

Notice that most of the commands in Fig. 7.4 require that you simultaneously press the control key *and* another key. Let's try moving through the
file.

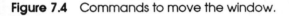

Ctrl *and* f	Forward one screen
Ctrl *and* b	Back one screen
Ctrl *and* d	Down (forward) one half-screen
Ctrl *and* u	Up (back) one half-screen
G	Go to the end of the file
nG	Go to line number n (n is a number)

Figure 7.4   Commands to move the window.

The commands $\boxed{\text{Ctrl}}$ *and* d and $\boxed{\text{Ctrl}}$ *and* u move through the file about a half-screen at a time. To see this, press

> $\boxed{\text{Ctrl}}$ *and* d

The screen will scroll, and the cursor will be positioned a partial screen down in the file, similar to the illustration in Fig. 7.5.

Again press

> $\boxed{\text{Ctrl}}$ *and* d

This time the text does not change because the last line of the file is already on the screen. However, the cursor will be positioned farther down the file as illustrated in Fig. 7.6.

Now move back up the file. Press

> $\boxed{\text{Ctrl}}$ *and* u

The cursor will move back up a partial screen, giving the same display as was illustrated in Fig. 7.5. Again press

> $\boxed{\text{Ctrl}}$ *and* u

```
Surveyor 1:Moon:US:66
Pioneer 7:Sun:US:66
Lunar Orbiter 2:Moon:US:66
Luna 13:Moon:USSR:66
Venera 4:Venus:USSR:67
Surveyor 5:Moon:US:67
Surveyor 6:Moon:US:67
Pioneer 8:Sun:US:67
Pioneer 9:Sun:US:67
Venera 5:Venus:USSR:69
Mariner 6:Mars:US:69
Venera 7:Venus:USSR:70
Luna 17:Moon:USSR:70
Mars 2:Mars:USSR:71
Mariner 9:Mars:US:71
Luna 19:Moon:USSR:71
Pioneer 10:Jupiter:US:72
Venera 8:Venus:USSR:72
Pioneer 11:Jupiter:US:73
Mariner 10:Venus:US:73
Viking 1:Mars:US:75
Voyager 2:Jupiter,Saturn:US:77
Voyager 1:Jupiter,Saturn,Uranus:US:77
```

Figure 7.5 The screen after moving down a partial screen (typical).

```
Surveyor 1:Moon:US:66
Pioneer 7:Sun:US:66
Lunar Orbiter 2:Moon:US:66
Luna 13:Moon:USSR:66
Venera 4:Venus:USSR:67
Surveyor 5:Moon:US:67
Surveyor 6:Moon:US:67
Pioneer 8:Sun:US:67
Pioneer 9:Sun:US:67
Venera 5:Venus:USSR:69
Mariner 6:Mars:US:69
Venera 7:Venus:USSR:70
Luna 17:Moon:USSR:70
Mars 2:Mars:USSR:71
Mariner 9:Mars:US:71
Luna 19:Moon:USSR:71
Pioneer 10:Jupiter:US:72
Venera 8:Venus:USSR:72
Pioneer 11:Jupiter:US:73
Mariner 10:Venus:US:73
Viking 1:Mars:US:75
Voyager 2:Jupiter,Saturn:US:77
Voyager 1:Jupiter,Saturn,Uranus:US:77
```

Figure 7.6 The screen after pressing Ctrl *and* d again (typical).

This time the screen does not scroll because the top line of the file is on the screen. However, the cursor will move up a partial screen. Again press

Ctrl *and* u

and the cursor will be positioned back at the top of the file.

To move through the file more quickly, you can use the commands Ctrl *and* f and Ctrl *and* b. Press

Ctrl *and* f

The window will scroll down an entire page. Since there is not another entire page of data in the file, part of the screen will be left with empty lines as indicated by the tildes (~) as shown in Fig. 7.7.

Now move back to the first page by pressing

Ctrl *and* b

The full screen of data, beginning with the first line, will be displayed as shown in Fig. 7.8. Notice the location of the cursor near the end of the screen.

118

```
Mariner 9:Mars:US:71
Luna 19:Moon:USSR:71
Pioneer 10:Jupiter:US:72
Venera 8:Venus:USSR:72
Pioneer 11:Jupiter:US:73
Mariner 10:Venus:US:73
Viking 1:Mars:US:75
Voyager 2:Jupiter,Saturn:US:77
Voyager 1:Jupiter,Saturn,Uranus:US:77
~
~
~
~
~
~
~
~
~
~
~
~
~
~
```

Figure 7.7 The screen after pressing (Ctrl) and f (typical).

```
Pioneer 1:Moon:US:58
Pioneer 4:Moon:US:59
Lunik 1:Moon:USSR:59
Ranger 7:Moon:US:64
Mariner 4:Mars:US:64
Venera 3:Venus:USSR:65
Pioneer 6:Moon:US:65
Surveyor 1:Moon:US:66
Pioneer 7:Sun:US:66
Lunar Orbiter 2:Moon:US:66
Luna 13:Moon:USSR:66
Venera 4:Venus:USSR:67
Surveyor 5:Moon:US:67
Surveyor 6:Moon:US:67
Pioneer 8:Sun:US:67
Pioneer 9:Sun:US:67
Venera 5:Venus:USSR:69
Mariner 6:Mars:US:69
Venera 7:Venus:USSR:70
Luna 17:Moon:USSR:70
Mars 2:Mars:USSR:71
Mariner 9:Mars:US:71
Luna 19:Moon:USSR:71
```

Figure 7.8 The screen after pressing (Ctrl) and b (typical).

Again press

Ctrl *and* b

This time you may hear a "beep" sound from the terminal, indicating that you are at the beginning of the file and cannot back up any further.

To move to a specific line in the file, you can use the G (goto) command. Notice that this is the *uppercase* G. Press

G

and vi will move the window to the end of the file and position the cursor to the last line. This is illustrated in Fig. 7.9.

You can move to a specific line in the file by pressing the line number *then* G. Press

2 *then* G

```
Surveyor 1:Moon:US:66
Pioneer 7:Sun:US:66
Lunar Orbiter 2:Moon:US:66
Luna 13:Moon:USSR:66
Venera 4:Venus:USSR:67
Surveyor 5:Moon:US:67
Surveyor 6:Moon:US:67
Pioneer 8:Sun:US:67
Pioneer 9:Sun:US:67
Venera 5:Venus:USSR:69
Mariner 6:Mars:US:69
Venera 7:Venus:USSR:70
Luna 17:Moon:USSR:70
Mars 2:Mars:USSR:71
Mariner 9:Mars:US:71
Luna 19:Moon:USSR:71
Pioneer 10:Jupiter:US:72
Venera 8:Venus:USSR:72
Pioneer 11:Jupiter:US:73
Mariner 10:Venus:US:73
Viking 1:Mars:US:75
Voyager 2:Jupiter,Saturn:US:77
Voyager 1:Jupiter,Saturn,Uranus:US:77
```

Figure 7.9   The G command moves to the end of the file (typical).

```
Pioneer 4:Moon:US:59
Lunik 1:Moon:USSR:59
Ranger 7:Moon:US:64
Mariner 4:Mars:US:64
Venera 3:Venus:USSR:65
Pioneer 6:Moon:US:65
Surveyor 1:Moon:US:66
Pioneer 7:Sun:US:66
Lunar Orbiter 2:Moon:US:66
Luna 13:Moon:USSR:66
Venera 4:Venus:USSR:67
Surveyor 5:Moon:US:67
Surveyor 6:Moon:US:67
Pioneer 8:Sun:US:67
Pioneer 9:Sun:US:67
Venera 5:Venus:USSR:69
Mariner 6:Mars:US:69
Venera 7:Venus:USSR:70
Luna 17:Moon:USSR:70
Mars 2:Mars:USSR:71
Mariner 9:Mars:US:71
Luna 19:Moon:USSR:71
Pioneer 10:Jupiter:US:72
```

Figure 7.10 The command 2G moves to the second line (typical).

and vi will move the window so that line 2 is on the screen and the cursor is positioned on that line. This is illustrated in Fig. 7.10.

Keystroke and Command Summary: Moving through the file

Vi commands:

Ctrl *and* f	forward one screen
Ctrl *and* b	back one screen
Ctrl *and* d	down (forward) one half-screen
Ctrl *and* u	up (back) one half-screen
G	go to the end of the file
n then G	go to line number *n* (*n* is a number)

What Can Go Wrong?

1. The commands to move the window do not work.

Cause: You might not have pressed the control key and the command character simultaneously. For example, Ctrl *and* f indicates that you hold down the control key and press f at the same time.

Solution: Be sure to hold down the control key when you use the commands to move the window.

2. The G command did not work.

Cause: Pressing lowercase g will not work. You must use uppercase G.

Solution: Press ⇧ and g.

Searching for Text

On occasion you might need to move the cursor to a specific line in the file but cannot use the G command because you do not know the line number. To locate a line on the basis of its content, you can use the commands shown in Fig. 7.11.

Take a look at your screen. The cursor should be located on the second line of the "allprobes" file. If it is not, press

> 2 *then* G

Now suppose that you need to move to a line in the file that contains the word "Jupiter." Enter

> /Jupiter

followed by ⏎. vi updates the window to contain the relevant line and moves the cursor to the beginning of the word Jupiter. This is shown in Fig. 7.12.

To repeat the search and locate the next line containing the word Jupiter, press

> n

and the screen will scroll down one line to the next occurrence of the word Jupiter. This is shown in Fig. 7.13.

/*text*	Search forward for the *text*
n	Repeat the previous search
?*text*	Search backward for the *text*
N	Repeat the previous search backward

Figure 7.11 Commands to search for text.

```
Pioneer 4:Moon:US:59
Lunik 1:Moon:USSR:59
Ranger 7:Moon:US:64
Mariner 4:Mars:US:64
Venera 3:Venus:USSR:65
Pioneer 6:Moon:US:65
Surveyor 1:Moon:US:66
Pioneer 7:Sun:US:66
Lunar Orbiter 2:Moon:US:66
Luna 13:Moon:USSR:66
Venera 4:Venus:USSR:67
Surveyor 5:Moon:US:67
Surveyor 6:Moon:US:67
Pioneer 8:Sun:US:67
Pioneer 9:Sun:US:67
Venera 5:Venus:USSR:69
Mariner 6:Mars:US:69
Venera 7:Venus:USSR:70
Luna 17:Moon:USSR:70
Mars 2:Mars:USSR:71
Mariner 9:Mars:US:71
Luna 19:Moon:USSR:71
Pioneer 10:Jupiter:US:72
/Jupiter
```

Figure 7.12 The screen after searching for Jupiter (typical).

```
Ranger 7:Moon:US:64
Mariner 4:Mars:US:64
Venera 3:Venus:USSR:65
Pioneer 6:Moon:US:65
Surveyor 1:Moon:US:66
Pioneer 7:Sun:US:66
Lunar Orbiter 2:Moon:US:66
Luna 13:Moon:USSR:66
Venera 4:Venus:USSR:67
Surveyor 5:Moon:US:67
Surveyor 6:Moon:US:67
Pioneer 8:Sun:US:67
Pioneer 9:Sun:US:67
Venera 5:Venus:USSR:69
Mariner 6:Mars:US:69
Venera 7:Venus:USSR:70
Luna 17:Moon:USSR:70
Mars 2:Mars:USSR:71
Mariner 9:Mars:US:71
Luna 19:Moon:USSR:71
Pioneer 10:Jupiter:US:72
Venera 8:Venus:USSR:72
Pioneer 11:Jupiter:US:73
```

Figure 7.13 The n command repeats the search (typical).

You can also search backward from the position of the cursor. To move to the previous line containing Jupiter, enter

    ?Jupiter

followed by ⏎. The cursor will move back to the line shown in Fig. 7.12.

> **Keystroke and Command Summary: Searching for text**
> Vi commands
>
> | | |
> |---|---|
> | /*text* | search forward for the text |
> | n | repeat the previous search |
> | ?*text* | search backward for the text |
> | N | repeat the previous search backward |
> | *n then* G | go to line number *n* |

What Can Go Wrong?

1. The search for Jupiter does not work.

Cause: You must be sure to spell Jupiter correctly and to use the uppercase J. Entering /jupiter will not work.

Solution: Enter /Jupiter ⏎ and be sure to use an uppercase J.

Some Convenient Shortcut Commands

You have already used the i and a commands in vi to enter insert mode. These lines begin inserting before and after the position of the cursor, respectively. As a convenience, vi provides the following shortcut commands for entering text at the beginning or end of the current line no matter where the cursor is located on that line.

I	insert text at the beginning of the line
A	insert text at the end of the line

Notice that these are the *uppercase* versions of the i and a commands. Before experimenting with these two commands, first move the cursor to the top of the file by pressing

    1 *then* G

Next press

    A

Notice that the cursor moves directly to the end of the first line and vi enters insert mode. You may now enter text. Enter

> :Successful

and leave the insert mode by pressing

> Esc

Next, add text to the beginning of that line. Press

> I

and notice that the cursor moves back to the beginning of the line; vi is now in insert mode. Enter

> United States

(enter a space after States) and leave insert mode by pressing

> Esc

The screen will now resemble Fig. 7.14 (typical).

```
United States Pioneer 1:Moon:US:58:Successful
Pioneer 4:Moon:US:59
Lunik 1:Moon:USSR:59
Ranger 7:Moon:US:64
Mariner 4:Mars:US:64
Venera 3:Venus:USSR:65
Pioneer 6:Moon:US:65
Surveyor 1:Moon:US:66
Pioneer 7:Sun:US:66
Lunar Orbiter 2:Moon:US:66
Luna 13:Moon:USSR:66
Venera 4:Venus:USSR:67
Surveyor 5:Moon:US:67
Surveyor 6:Moon:US:67
Pioneer 8:Sun:US:67
Pioneer 9:Sun:US:67
Venera 5:Venus:USSR:69
Mariner 6:Mars:US:69
Venera 7:Venus:USSR:70
Luna 17:Moon:USSR:70
Mars 2:Mars:USSR:71
Mariner 9:Mars:US:71
Luna 19:Moon:USSR:71
```

Figure 7.14 The screen after using A and I to insert text.

A shortcut command to move the cursor to the beginning of the line (but not enter insert mode) is the 0 (zero) command. Press

0

and notice that the cursor moves to the beginning of the line.

Now enter the command

d *then* w

and notice that the word "United" is deleted. The command **dw** means "delete word."

vi also supports another shortcut that can be used on many commands that you already know. If you need to execute a command a number of times in a row, you simply enter the number, called the **repetition count**, followed by the command. For example, suppose that you want to delete the word "States" and the space that follows it. You could use dw or press x seven times. Using the repetition count, enter

7 *then* x

and vi will repeat the x command seven times (removing the States and the space that follows it). The repetition count can be used on many other vi commands, including the cursor positioning commands, and the dd (line delete) command.

Now quickly move the cursor to the end of the line by pressing

$

Back up the cursor ten times by entering

10 *then* h

The cursor should now be under the colon before the word "Successful" as shown in Fig. 7.15.

A shortcut that will delete all of the text from the cursor to the end of the line is the D command. Press

D

to delete the text ":Successful."

> **Keystroke and Command Summary: Some convenient shortcut commands**
>
> A   insert text at the end of the line
>
> D   delete to end of line
>
> I   insert text at the beginning of the line
>
> 0 (zero) move the cursor to the beginning of the current line

```
Pioneer 1:Moon:US:58:Successful
Pioneer 4:Moon:US:59
Lunik 1:Moon:USSR:59
Ranger 7:Moon:US:64
Mariner 4:Mars:US:64
Venera 3:Venus:USSR:65
Pioneer 6:Moon:US:65
Surveyor 1:Moon:US:66
Pioneer 7:Sun:US:66
Lunar Orbiter 2:Moon:US:66
Luna 13:Moon:USSR:66
Venera 4:Venus:USSR:67
Surveyor 5:Moon:US:67
Surveyor 6:Moon:US:67
Pioneer 8:Sun:US:67
Pioneer 9:Sun:US:67
Venera 5:Venus:USSR:69
Mariner 6:Mars:US:69
Venera 7:Venus:USSR:70
Luna 17:Moon:USSR:70
Mars 2:Mars:USSR:71
Mariner 9:Mars:US:71
Luna 19:Moon:USSR:71
```

Figure 7.15 The cursor position after the $ and 10h commands (typical).

$	move the cursor to the end of the current line
dw	delete a word
n then x	do the x command *n* times
n then h	do the h command *n* times

What Can Go Wrong?

1. The A or I command does not work.

Cause: You might have entered these commands in lowercase.

Solution: Be sure to hold the shift key down when using the A and I commands.

Copying and Moving Lines

Occasionally, you might need to rearrange the contents of a file or duplicate a portion of the text. Duplication is sometimes convenient when you are preparing a file of test data for a program or entering a portion of text that is very similar to some existing data in the file. Figure 7.16 lists commands that can be used for copying and moving text. Both the dd and the Y (uppercase Y) commands can be preceded by a repetition count to delete or yank more than a single line.

Let's investigate these commands. The cursor should be on the first line of the file. If it is not, enter

　　1 *then* G

Now yank the three lines of data about launches in the 1950s by entering

　　3 *then* Y

The screen does not change, but the three lines have been copied into a buffer in vi. A **buffer** is some memory in vi that will temporarily hold information. You can copy these lines to the bottom of the file by first moving the cursor there and then using the p command. First, enter

　　G

to move to the end of the file. The cursor will now be on the last line of the file. To copy the "yanked" lines out of the buffer, press

　　p

(lowercase p) to put these lines after the line where the cursor is located. The screen will now appear as shown in Fig. 7.17.

Notice that vi displays the first of the copied lines (Pioneer 1) and the message 3 more lines on the command line. The other two copied lines are thus below the window. To see them, press

　　Ctrl *and* d

d *then* d	delete one or more lines and save them in the buffer
Y	copy (yank) one or more lines into the buffer
y *then* y	same as Y
p	copy text from the buffer after the current line
P	copy text from the buffer above the current line

Figure 7.16 Commands for copying and moving text.

```
Pioneer 7:Sun:US:66
Lunar Orbiter 2:Moon:US:66
Luna 13:Moon:USSR:66
Venera 4:Venus:USSR:67
Surveyor 5:Moon:US:67
Surveyor 6:Moon:US:67
Pioneer 8:Sun:US:67
Pioneer 9:Sun:US:67
Venera 5:Venus:USSR:69
Mariner 6:Mars:US:69
Venera 7:Venus:USSR:70
Luna 17:Moon:USSR:70
Mars 2:Mars:USSR:71
Mariner 9:Mars:US:71
Luna 19:Moon:USSR:71
Pioneer 10:Jupiter:US:72
Venera 8:Venus:USSR:72
Pioneer 11:Jupiter:US:73
Mariner 10:Venus:US:73
Viking 1:Mars:US:75
Voyager 2:Jupiter,Saturn:US:77
Voyager 1:Jupiter,Saturn,Uranus:US:77
Pioneer 1:Moon:US:58
3 more lines
```

Figure 7.17 The first three lines copied to the end of the file (typical).

Now move back to the top of the file by pressing

> 1 *then* G

Next, you will *move* the first two lines of the file to another place in the file. Enter

> 2 *then* d *then* d

This will delete the first two lines from the file and automatically save them in the "yank" buffer. Let's place these lines after the launches from the 1960s. To move the cursor to the first of the 1970's launches, search for Venera 7 by entering

> /Venera 7

followed by ⏎. To put the deleted lines above this line, press

> P

(uppercase P). Notice that vi inserts the deleted lines above Venera 7, as illustrated in Fig. 7.18.

```
Lunik 1:Moon:USSR:59
Ranger 7:Moon:US:64
Mariner 4:Mars:US:64
Venera 3:Venus:USSR:65
Pioneer 6:Moon:US:65
Surveyor 1:Moon:US:66
Pioneer 7:Sun:US:66
Lunar Orbiter 2:Moon:US:66
Luna 13:Moon:USSR:66
Venera 4:Venus:USSR:67
Surveyor 5:Moon:US:67
Surveyor 6:Moon:US:67
Pioneer 8:Sun:US:67
Pioneer 9:Sun:US:67
Venera 5:Venus:USSR:69
Mariner 6:Mars:US:69
Pioneer 1:Moon:US:58
Pioneer 4:Moon:US:59
Venera 7:Venus:USSR:70
Luna 17:Moon:USSR:70
Mars 2:Mars:USSR:71
Mariner 9:Mars:US:71
Luna 19:Moon:USSR:71
```

Figure 7.18 Screen after moving 2 lines (typical).

You will notice that the P or p command only inserted the last group of deleted or yanked lines; previously deleted or yanked lines in the buffer are lost. Also, we used the first two or three lines from the file for illustration purposes; the method of copying and deleting lines will work for any lines in the file. Finally, if you accidentally delete one or more lines, you can use P (or u) immediately afterward to restore the deletion.

> **Keystroke and Command Summary: Copying and moving lines**
> Vi commands
>
> dd   delete one or more lines and save them in the buffer
>
> Y   copy (yank) one or more lines into the buffer
>
> yy   same as Y
>
> p   put the text in the buffer after the current line
>
> P   put the text in the buffer above the current line

What Can Go Wrong?

1. The yank command did not work.

Cause: You might have entered lowercase y.

Solution: Be sure to hold the shift key down when using the yank command.

Changing Multiple Lines

You will on occasion need to change every occurrence of some text in a file. For example, suppose that you decided to change the text in the "all-probes" file from "US" to "United States." To do this, you can use the substitute command, which is entered on vi's command line. The syntax for the substitute command is

> *[first line, last line]s/old text/new text/*⏎

The "first line,last line" is called the **range**. If you don't specify a range, the substitute command applies to the current line where the cursor is located. Let's look at an example. Position the cursor to the second line of the file by pressing

> 2 *then* G

This is the line for Ranger 7, since the original first two lines were moved in the last section. Now use the substitute command to change the text "US:" to "United States:". First, move to the vi command line by pressing

> :

Then enter the substitute command

> s/US:/United States:/

followed by ⏎. This makes the substitution on the current line. The screen should appear as shown in Fig. 7.19.

To change "US:" to "United States:" on all the rest of the lines in the file, press

> :

to move to the command line, and enter:

> 3,$s/US:/United States:/

followed by ⏎. The range 3,$ means from line 3 through the last line of the file. (The $ is shorthand for the last line of the file.) The screen will scroll and display the last screen of the file, as shown in Fig. 7.20.

```
Lunik 1:Moon:USSR:59
Ranger 7:Moon:United States:64
Mariner 4:Mars:US:64
Venera 3:Venus:USSR:65
Pioneer 6:Moon:US:65
Surveyor 1:Moon:US:66
Pioneer 7:Sun:US:66
Lunar Orbiter 2:Moon:US:66
Luna 13:Moon:USSR:66
Venera 4:Venus:USSR:67
Surveyor 5:Moon:US:67
Surveyor 6:Moon:US:67
Pioneer 8:Sun:US:67
Pioneer 9:Sun:US:67
Venera 5:Venus:USSR:69
Mariner 6:Mars:US:69
Pioneer 1:Moon:US:58
Pioneer 4:Moon:US:59
Venera 7:Venus:USSR:70
Luna 17:Moon:USSR:70
Mars 2:Mars:USSR:71
Mariner 9:Mars:US:71
Luna 19:Moon:USSR:71
:s/US:/United States:/
```

Figure 7.19   A typical screen after using the substitute command.

You can verify that all of the appropriate lines have been changed by pressing

> [Ctrl] *and* b

to move back one screen.

> **Keystroke and Command Summary: Changing multiple lines**
> Vi commands
>
> > :[*first line,last line*]s/*old text*/*new text*/⏎
>
> Substitute the *new text* for the *old text* on each line of the specified range.

```
Mariner 9:Mars:United States:71
Luna 19:Moon:USSR:71
Pioneer 10:Jupiter:United States:72
Venera 8:Venus:USSR:72
Pioneer 11:Jupiter:United States:73
Mariner 10:Venus:United States:73
Viking 1:Mars:United States:75
Voyager 2:Jupiter,Saturn:United States:77
Voyager 1:Jupiter,Saturn,Uranus:United States:77
Pioneer 1:Moon:United States:58
Pioneer 4:Moon:United States:59
Lunik 1:Moon:USSR:59
~
~
~
~
~
~
~
~
~
~
~
~
```

Figure 7.20 A typical screen after using the substitute command again.

What Can Go Wrong?

1. Lines with "US" and "USSR" were modified.

Cause: You might have left the colon out of the text on the substitute command. If you enter s/US/United States/, all lines with either "US" or "USSR" will match the old text and thus will be modified.

Solution: Be sure to include the colons as shown below:

    s/US:/United States:/

2. After you copied or moved lines, the cursor moved erratically, and the screen did not appear as shown in the text.

Cause: A transmission error might have caused some of vi's output to be lost.

Solution: From within vi, press

    Ctrl and l

(lowercase "ell"). This is the vi command to refresh your screen.

Reading and Writing Files

Another useful command that is entered on vi's command line is the **r** (read) command. This command is useful for copying the contents of an existing file into another. To illustrate, move to the end of your file by pressing

G

Now copy the contents of the file "probes.60" into the "allprobes" file by entering

    :r probes.60

followed by ⏎. This command inserts the contents of the file "probes.60" after the current line.

You can write the current file out to another file by using the **w** (write) command. This is sometimes useful when you have made many changes to a file and you don't want to overwrite the old version of the file. To write the current file out to a file called junk, enter

    :w junk

followed by ⏎. This will save all of the changes that you have made thus far, but it will preserve the original version of the "allprobes" file.

Now leave vi by entering the command:

    :q!

followed by ⏎. The **q!** command tells vi to quit immediately without writing out the updated file. This will preserve the original contents of the file "allprobes."

> **Keystroke and Command Summary: Reading and writing files**
> Vi commands
>
> :r *filename* ⏎   insert the contents of the named file after the current line
>
> :w *filename* ⏎   write the current file out to the given filename
>
> :q! ⏎   quit (exit) vi without saving changes

What Can Go Wrong?

1. When you entered the command :r probes.60 vi responded with a message similar to

    "probes.60" No such file or directory

Cause: Vi could not find the file "probes.60" in the current directory.

Solution: Reenter the command and be sure to spell the file name correctly.

Recovering an Editing Session after a Crash

If you have a considerable amount of editing to perform on a file, it is a good practice to save your changes every 15 minutes or so. Every 15 minutes or so, with vi in command mode, enter : *then* w. This command will write out your current changes and keep you in vi. This way, if the UNIX system crashes, you will minimize the amount of possible data that might be lost.

As a fail-safe mechanism, vi has the ability to recover most of your changes should a crash occur and you have not saved your file as described above. If you are in vi when the system crashes or if your workstation is unexpectedly disconnected from the UNIX system, you might be able to recover most of your changes the next time that you log into the system by changing to the same directory that you were in at the time of the crash and entering the command

```
vi -r filename
```

where "filename" is the name of the file that you were editing. The option -r means recover; vi will recover as many changes as possible.

This completes Chapter 7. At this time you should log out of your system and review the topics in this chapter by completing the self-test at the end of the chapter.

┃ Command Summary

Vi Commands

Ctrl *and* f	forward one screen
Ctrl *and* b	back one screen
Ctrl *and* d	down (forward) one half screen
Ctrl *and* u	up (back) one half screen
Ctrl *and* l	refresh the screen
/*text*	search forward for the *text*
n	repeat the previous search
?*text*	search backward for the *text*

N	repeat the previous search backward
G	go to the end of the file
n then G	go to line number *n*
A	insert text at the end of the line
I	insert text at the beginning of the line
0 (zero)	move the cursor to the beginning of the current line
$	move the cursor to the end of the current line
D	delete to end of line
dw	delete a word
n then x	do the x command *n* times
n then h	do the h command *n* times
dd	delete one or more lines and save them in the buffer
Y	copy (yank) one or more lines into the buffer
yy	same as Y
p	put the text in the buffer after the current line
P	put the text in the buffer above the current line
:[*first line,last line*]s/*old text*/*new text*/⏎	substitute *new text* for *old text* between lines *first line* and *last line*
:r *filename* ⏎	insert the contents of the named file after the current line
:w [*filename*]⏎	write the current file out to the given filename (or current file)
:q! ⏎	quit immediately without saving any changes made since the last write

UNIX Commands

cat *file* display the contents of a file

cd *directory* change the current working directory

ls list file names in the current directory

vi -r *filename* recover an edit session

Self-Test

1. List all of the vi commands from this and previous chapters that will cause vi to enter insert mode. _____ i a o O A I

2. Suppose the cursor is positioned under the O in "Lunar Orbiter" as shown below:

   Lunar Orbiter 2:Moon:US:66

   List two different commands that can be used to delete the word "Orbiter" and its trailing space: ___dw___ and _____

3. In the spaces below, compose the vi command to perform the stated functions:

   __/Saturn__ a. a command to search forward in a file for the word "Saturn"

   __?Sun__ b. a command to search backward in a file for the word "Sun"

   __1G__ c. a command to move the cursor to the first line of the file, no matter what its current position

   __A__ d. a command to move the cursor to the end of the current line and enter insert mode

   __G__ e. a command to position the cursor to the end of the file, no matter what its current position

4. Suppose the cursor is positioned under the O in "Lunar Orbiter" as shown below:

   Lunar Orbiter 2:Moon:US:66

   List two different commands that can be used to move the cursor to the beginning *of that line*: ___0___ and ___bh___

5. Suppose the cursor is positioned on the first line of the "allprobes" file. Write a sequence of four commands that could be used to move the second and third lines of that file to the end of the file: ___j___, __2dd__, ___G___, and

   __p__

6. Repeat question 5 but instead of moving the two lines, copy them. j 2Y G p

7. The name for the Y command is ___yank___.

8. Suppose that you need to change all of the years in the file "probes.70" to include the century. That is, 70 should be changed to 1970, 71 to 1971, 72 to 1972, and so on. Compose a single vi command that will accomplish this: __:1,$s/:7/:19?__

9. Suppose that you are editing the file "probes.60" and you have made a lot of changes. You want to save the changes, but you do not want to overwrite the

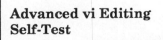

Advanced vi Editing
Self-Test

137

original file. Compose a command that will save the changes in a file called "probes.new" and a second command that will then immediately exit vi without overwriting "probes.60": ___:w probes.new___ and ___:q!___

10. Suppose that you want to create a file to hold probes from both the 1970s and 1980s. You have created a new file using the command

    vi probes.80

and now you want to copy into that file all of the data from the file "probes.70." Compose a command that will accomplish this: ____:r probes.70____

11. True or false: You have been editing with vi for an hour, and you have not saved your file. The system crashes. You have now lost all of your changes.

12. List vi commands presented in this chapter that must be terminated by pressing ⏎: _____

Exercises

1. For this exercise you will use the telephone directory file and the phone subdirectory that you created in previous chapter exercises. Perform the following vi operations on your file. Record the commands that you used.

   a. Search for a particular name.

   b. Move the cursor to the end of the file.

   c. Search backward for a particular name.

   d. With a single command, position the cursor to the third line of the file. Assume that the cursor could be anywhere in file.

   e. With a single command, position the cursor to the top of the file. Assume that the cursor could be anywhere in file.

   f. Copy five lines of text into the buffer.

   g. Move to the end of the file.

   h. Put the contents of the buffer into the end of the file.

   i. Enter the command 4p to put the contents of the buffer into the file four more times.

   j. Use the commands Ctrl and f, Ctrl and b, Ctrl and d, Ctrl and u to move around the file.

   k. Exit the file without saving the above changes.

8

UNIX System Communications

This chapter:

- describes how to share files with other users

- presents the write command for interactive communication

- presents the mail command for E-mail

Users on a UNIX system are often involved in team projects such as writing individual chapters for a book or writing individual modules for a large programming project. Team efforts require the exchange of information. This chapter presents three ways to communicate with other users on a UNIX system. These are (1) sharing files, (2) sending messages to other logged-on users, and (3) sending electronic mail to other users. Let's first look at ways to share files.

Sharing Files

Team projects often lead to situations in which you need to give a copy of one of your files to another person. For example, you might have written a portion of a report

```
$ cd launches
$ cp allprobes /usr/acct/bakers/allprobes.new
$
```

Figure 8.1   Sharing a file with another user.

that is to be combined with the work of others to form the final paper. It
would be convenient to bring all of the individual portions of the report into a
single directory and merge them together there. This section will describe
how this might be accomplished via examples from the author's UNIX system.

You know that each user on the system has his or her own home directory
and that these directories are (typically) all subdirectories of same parent
directory. This was illustrated in Fig. 4.1 in Chapter 4. This organization
makes it easy to exchange files with other users on the same UNIX system.
For example, a friend of mine (Sarah) uses the home directory "/usr/acct/
bakers" and my home directory is "/usr/acct/troyd." Suppose Sarah would like
a copy of my file named "allprobes." The commands shown in Fig. 8.1 will
copy my "allprobes" file (from the "launches" subdirectory) to the file
"allprobes.new" within Sarah's "/usr/acct/bakers" directory, assuming that
her directory has permissions that allow this. The cp command in Fig. 8.1 is
explained in Fig. 8.2.

The act of copying files into another user's directory implies a cooperative
community of users. Unauthorized copying of files is viewed as improper. If
necessary, you can deny users the opportunity to copy files into your directory
by removing the w permission from that directory. This was discussed in
Chapter 6.

The example in Fig. 8.1 illustrates one way in which I could give a copy of
one of my files to another user (Sarah). With Sarah's permission I could copy
her file named "allprobes" from her "launches" subdirectory into a file named
"allprobes.new" in my current directory by using the command

       cp /usr/acct/bakers/launches/allprobes allprobes.new

                          ┌─ Existing file to be copied
            cp allprobes /usr/acct/bakers/allprobes.new
                         └─────┬─────┘   │
Directory path for the new file ─────┘   │
                                         └── Name of (new) copied file

Figure 8.2   Explanation of the cp command.

This command uses the full path name of Sarah's "allprobes" file as the old file and copies this into a new file named "allprobes.new" in my current working directory.

To restrict a user from taking files out of your directories, you can remove your directory's x permission. This was also discussed in Chapter 6.

> **Keystroke and Command Summary: Sharing files**
>
> UNIX commands
>
> cp *filename pathname*   copy the *filename* to another user using the specified *pathname*
>
> cp *pathname filename*   copy the file specified by the given *pathname* to the *filename* in the current directory

What Can Go Wrong?

1. When you use the cp command to copy a file to another user, the user does not find the file.

Cause: You have an error in the destination path name.

Solution: Verify the path name. Verify the destination user's complete directory path name.

2. When you attempt to copy a file to another user, you receive the message

    cp: cannot create

Cause: The other user has removed the w (write) permission from his or her directory.

Solution: You must ask the other user to restore the write permission until you have copied the file into that user's directory.

3. When you attempt to copy a file from another user, you receive the message

    cp: cannot access

Cause: The other user has removed the x (execute) permission from his or her directory.

Solution: You must ask the other user to set the execute permission until you have copied the file into your directory.

Communicating with Logged-on Users

The preceding section described ways to share entire files of information. Another method of communication is to send short interactive messages to other logged-on users in a manner similar to CB radio.

To try this, go to your UNIX system and log into your account. Next, find out who is currently logged on by entering the command

```
who
```

The typical output of the who command on the author's system is shown in Fig. 8.3.

The login-ids are shown in the first column of the output. You can communicate interactively with the users who are logged into your system by using the command **write**.

The syntax for the write command is

```
write login-id
```

where "*login-id*" is one of the id's shown in the output of the who command. In order for the other user to send messages back to you, he or she would also enter a write command specifying your login id.

You can try out the write command by communicating with yourself. Enter the command

```
write your-login-id
```

where *your-login-id* is *your* personal login-id. After you enter the write command, you will see a message similar to the following displayed on your screen:

```
Message from troyd (tty06) [Mon Jan 20 13:32:48] ...
```

This is the message that the user to whom you are writing would receive. After this, anything that you type will be sent by the write command to the indicated user, in this case *you*.

Notice that the UNIX prompt does not appear when you are within the write command. Anything that you type is immediately sent to the user with whom you are communicating. Try it. Enter a line of text and press ⏎. Notice that each message that you enter appears twice: once when you enter it and

```
$who
troyd     tty01     Jan 20     13:30
bakers    tty09     Jan 20     11:21
$
```

Figure 8.3 Typical output of the who command.

142

```
$ write troyd
    Message from troyd (tty06) [Mon Jan 20 13:32:48] ...
This is a message to myself
This is a message to myself
o
o
I hate talking to myself
I hate talking to myself
Bye!
Bye!
oo
oo
EOF
$
```

Figure 8.4 A sample conversation using write (typical display).

again after it is sent back to yourself by the write command. If you were communicating with someone else (instead of yourself), you would see only the first instance of each line. A sample session using write is illustrated in Fig. 8.4.

Think about how pilots and truckers communicate over radio. After expressing a thought or question, they usually say "over" or "back to you" to indicate to the other party that they are waiting for a response. UNIX users follow a similar convention when using the write command. Look at Fig. 8.4. By convention, a user who is ready for a response will enter

o

meaning "over." A user who is completely finished will enter

oo

meaning "over and out."

To exit from the write command, you must enter Ctrl *and* d. When you press control-d, the write command will display

EOF

(or possibly EOT) and return to the shell prompt. This is illustrated on the second-to-last line in Fig. 8.4. Notice that "EOF" is not entered by the user. It is displayed by the write command when you press Ctrl *and* d. At this time, press Ctrl *and* d.

You use the **mesg** command to prohibit other users from writing to you. The syntax is

mesg [n] [y]

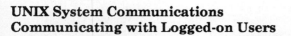

The argument n means no (disallow writing to you) and y means yes (allow writing). If you have a friend who is in the habit of interrupting you with the write command while you are editing, you might find the mesg command useful.

> **Keystroke and Command Summary: Communicating with logged-on users**
>
> UNIX commands
>
> | | |
> |---|---|
> | mesg [n] [y] | allow and disallow writing to you |
> | write *login-id* | communicate in real time with a currently logged-on user |
> | Ctrl *and* d | terminate a write session |

What Can Go Wrong?

1. When you attempt to write to someone else, you receive the message

```
login-id not logged in.
```

where "*login-id*" is the id of the user to whom you are attempting to write.

Cause: That user is not logged in.

Solution: You must wait until that person logs in or use the UNIX electronic mail (see the next section). Enter the who command to find out who is logged in.

2. After entering the write command, you cannot get back to the shell prompt.

Cause: You have not properly exited from write.

Solution: To exit the write command, press

Ctrl *and* d

Electronic Mail

Sending Mail

The write command is restricted to users who are logged into the system at the same time. To communicate with a user who is not currently logged in, you can use UNIX **electronic mail**. Electronic mail allows you to compose and send messages to other users on your UNIX system and in some cases to users on other systems. Unlike messages sent with the write command, electronic mail messages are not immediately displayed on the recipient's screen but are stored in a file called a **mailbox** until that user decides to read the message.

There are two widely used versions of mail: the **original mail** distributed with System V and an **enhanced mail**, which is distributed on Berkeley versions and also on many System V versions, where it is called **mailx**. Both versions operate in a similar manner, but enhanced mail has some additional commands and features. Both versions will be introduced in this section.

You can determine the version of mail on your system by starting the mail command. Enter the command

```
mail login-id
```

where *login-id* is *your* login-id. (To send mail to other users, you must ask them for their login-ids and use those with the mail command.) Depending on the version of mail, your screen will appear as shown in Fig. 8.5a or Fig. 8.5b. (My login-id is used in the figures; substitute yours in its place.)

Notice the difference in the response of the mail command in Figs. 8.5a and 8.5b. After you enter the mail command, original mail silently waits for you to enter a mail message; enhanced mail displays the prompt Subject?. Notice which version of mail you are using. On System V you might have both mail and mailx. If so, you will have to use the mailx command to use the enhanced mail.

If you are using enhanced mail, enter the subject

```
test number 1
```

and press ⏎. The cursor will move to the next line and will wait for the text for a mail message, as in original mail.

```
$ mail troyd

—
```

Figure 8.5(a)   Typical response from original mail in send mode.

```
$ mail troyd
Subject?_
```

Figure 8.5(b)   Typical response from enhanced mail in send mode.

```
$ mail troyd
Subject? test number 1
I have decided what model of car to buy. Now I
have to decide the options that I want.
How do you like your sun roof? Send an answer via E-mail.

—
```

Figure 8.6 A sample mail message (typical display).

Now (for both versions of mail) enter the text of a message. You can enter a message like the one shown in Fig. 8.6 or use one of your own. Please notice that Fig. 8.6 was produced by using enhanced mail. If you are using original mail, you will not have a subject line.

Examine Fig. 8.6. You will notice that mail does not issue prompts for your message. You simply enter the text of your message, a line at a time, pressing ⏎ when it is convenient to move to another line. (Lines don't have to end with periods.) When you are composing a message as illustrated above, we say that mail is in **send mode**.

After composing your message, you can then send it. To do so, press

⏎

after the last line. Now *with the cursor on a line by itself*, as shown in Fig. 8.6, press

Ctrl *and* d

At this point, some versions of enhanced mail will respond with the prompt

Cc:

meaning "complimentary copy." At this prompt you may enter another login-id for a person whom you would like to have receive a copy of your message or just press ⏎ for no complimentary copy. For our example, if you see the Cc: prompt, just press

⏎

to indicate no complimentary copies. The mail command will now silently deliver the mail message to the recipient's (in this case your own) mailbox. After sending the message your system should return to the shell prompt.

Now send a second message to yourself. You can follow the example in Fig. 8.7, but substitute your own login-id in place of mine. If you see the Subject? prompt, enter a subject line. After composing your message, remember to press Ctrl *and* d on a line by itself to terminate and send the message. If you see the Cc: prompt, press ⏎.

```
$ mail troyd
Subject? test number 2
This is the second message that I have sent
to myself!
$ _
```

Figure 8.7 A second mail message.

> **Keyword and Command Summary: Sending mail**
>
> UNIX commands
>
> mail *login-id*   send messages to a user's mailbox
>
> Mail send mode commands
>
> Ctrl *and* d   end and send a mail message

What Can Go Wrong?

1. After you compose a mail message and press Ctrl *and* d, nothing happens.

Cause: You did not enter Ctrl *and* d on a line by itself.

Solution: Be sure to enter Ctrl *and* d on a line by itself. Try this. If you still have trouble, an alternative way to terminate and send the message is to enter a single period on a line by itself then press ↵ at the end of the message.

2. After you compose a mail message using enhanced mail and press Ctrl *and* d, you receive the message

        No recipients specified

Cause: You did not specify a login-id on the mail command line.

Solution: Be sure to specify a login-id on the command line.

3. After you compose a mail message and press Ctrl *and* d, you receive one of the following messages:

        login-id...User unknown

or

        mail: Can't send to login-id
            Mail saved in dead.letter

Cause: The login-id that you used on the mail command is not the login-id of a known user on the system.

Solution: You must use a known login-id. You must get the correct login-id from another user of the system.

Receiving Mail

When you receive mail in your mailbox file, you will be notified by the UNIX system through the following (or similar) message

```
You have mail
```

This message will be displayed after completing your next command if the mail arrives when you are logged in. If the mail is delivered while you are logged off, the message will be displayed the next time that you log on. In either case you can leave the mail in the mailbox until it is convenient to read it.

To read your mail, you use the command mode of the mail command. Original mail and enhanced mail operate differently in command mode, so this section has two subsections: one for original mail and the other for enhanced mail. Read the section that is appropriate for your system.

Receiving Mail: Original Mail

Read this subsection if you are using original mail.

To read mail messages from your mailbox, at the shell prompt enter

```
mail
```

and you will see a response similar to Fig. 8.8.

Original mail first displays the most recent (newest) message delivered into your mailbox and then presents the ? prompt. (*Note:* Some versions of mail may use the & character for the command prompt.) Notice in Fig. 8.8 that the mail system adds a header to each message that tells you the author of the message and the date and time that it was sent. Mail is now in *command mode* and is awaiting a mail command.

To view each message in the mailbox, simply press ⏎ at the prompt. Original mail will move through the mailbox from the newest to the oldest message. Following our example, the output will be similar to that shown in Fig. 8.9.

Again, press

⏎

```
$ mail
From troyd Tue Jun  6 09:40 EDT 1989
This is the second message that I have sent
to myself!
?
```

Figure 8.8 Typical original mail in command mode.

148

```
$ mail
From troyd Tue Jun  6 09:40 EDT 1989
This is the second message that I have sent
to myself!
?
From troyd Tue Jun  6 09:31 EDT 1989
I have decided what model of car to buy. Now I
have to decide the options that I want.
How do you like your sun roof? Send an answer via E-mail.
?
```

Figure 8.9 Next (older) message displayed by original mail after pressing ⏎.

Since there are no more messages in the mailbox, original mail will exit mail, and your system will return to the shell prompt. Both mail messages are saved in the mailbox.

With the shell prompt on the screen, reenter mail by entering

    `mail`

Again, the newest message in the mailbox will be displayed as shown in Fig. 8.8, and the mail prompt will be displayed on the screen. The last message on the screen is called the *current message*. Figure 8.10 lists some of the commands that you can enter at the prompt, many of which operate on the current message.

You should now have the mail prompt on your screen. Press

    `d`

to delete the current message. Next, press

    `q`

to leave mail. This sequence of commands will delete one message from the mailbox, leave the other message unharmed, and exit to the shell, as illustrated in Fig. 8.11.

d	delete the current message
⏎	display the next message
p	display the current message again
q	quit the mail command
s [*file*]	save the current message in the named *file*
?	help; display a list of all mail commands

Figure 8.10 Some original mail commands.

```
$ mail
From troyd Tue Jun  6 09:27 EDT 1989
This is the second message that I have sent
to myself!
?d
?q
$
```

Figure 8.11   Deleting a mail message in original mail.

Again, at the shell prompt, enter

    mail

and original mail will display the newest (in this case the only) message in your mailbox. At the mail prompt, enter

    d

to delete this message. Mail will exit and return to the shell prompt, since there are no other messages in the mailbox.

Enter the mail command again:

    mail

and you should see the message

    No mail.

since all of the mail messages in the mailbox have been deleted. Your shell prompt should be displayed.

The other commands in Fig. 8.10 are used less frequently. The p command will redisplay the current message. This is useful for long messages that scroll off the screen. To stop the message partway through the output, press your system's interrupt key. The ? command gives you help by listing the mail commands.

This concludes the introduction to original mail. Skip ahead to the Keystroke and Command Summary for this section if you are using original mail.

Receiving Mail: Enhanced Mail

Read this subsection if you are using enhanced mail.

To read mail from your mailbox, at the shell prompt enter

    mail

and you will see a response similar to Fig. 8.12.

Enhanced mail first displays a one-line header for each message in the mailbox, then presents the ? prompt. (*Note:* Some versions of mail may use the & character for the command prompt.) The display in Fig. 8.12 indicates that there are two messages in the mailbox. Mail is now in *command mode* and is awaiting a mail command.

```
$ mail
mail version 2.18 7/1/89.  Type ? for help.
>N   1 troyd      Tue Jun  6 09:31   8/190  test number 1
 N   2 troyd      Tue Jun  6 09:40   7/127  test number 2
?
```

Figure 8.12 Enhanced mail in command mode (typical).

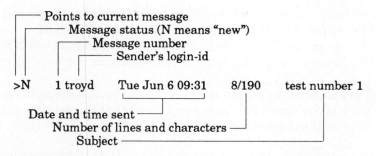

Figure 8.13 Description of the header line.

The header gives you information about each mail message. The header is explained in Fig. 8.13.

To view each message in the mailbox, simply press the message number followed by  at the prompt. For example, to view message number 1, press

1

and ⏎. The output will be similar to that shown in Fig. 8.14.

```
$ mail
mail version 2.18 7/1/89.  Type ? for help.
>N   1 troyd      Tue Jun  6 09:31   8/190  test number 1
 N   2 troyd      Tue Jun  6 09:40   7/127  test number 2
?1
Message  1:
From troyd Tue June  6 09:31 EDT 1989
To: troyd
Subject: test number 1
Status: R

I have decided what model of car to buy. Now I
have to decide the options that I want.
How do you like your sun roof? Send an answer via E-mail.
?
```

Figure 8.14 First message displayed by enhanced mail after pressing ⏎.

Notice in Fig. 8.14 that mail adds a header to each message that tells you the message number, author, date and time the message was sent, and status of the message.

Now press

⏎

and you will see the next message displayed. Pressing ⏎ at the mail prompt will display the message with the next highest message number. Again, press

⏎

This time no more messages are displayed because you are at the end of your mailbox. The output from these commands is shown in Fig. 8.15.

Notice that as you read messages, their status is changed from N ("new") to R ("read"). The status lets you know which messages you have already read.

The last message on the screen is called the **current message**. Figure 8.16 lists some of the commands that you can enter at the prompt, many of which operate on the current message.

```
$ mail
mail version 2.18 7/1/89.  Type ? for help.
>N   1 troyd     Tue Jun  6 09:31   8/190  test number 1
 N   2 troyd     Tue Jun  6 09:40   7/127  test number 2
?1
Message   1:
From troyd Tue June  6 09:31 EDT 1989
To: troyd
Subject: test number 1
Status: R


I have decided what model of car to buy. Now I
have to decide the options that I want.
How do you like your sun roof? Send an answer via E-mail.
?⏎
From troyd Tue Jun  6  09:40 EDT 1989
To: troyd
Subject: test number 2
Status: R


This is the second message that I have sent
to myself!
?⏎
At EOF
?
```

Figure 8.15 Moving through the mailbox (typical).

d	delete the current message
⏎	display the next message
p	display the current message again
q	quit the mail command
s [*file*]	save the current message in the named *file*
?	help; display a list of all mail commands

Figure 8.16 Some enhanced mail commands.

You should now have the mail prompt on your screen. Press

        d

to delete the current message (message number 2). Next, press

        q

to leave mail. This sequence of commands will delete one message from the mailbox, leave the other message unharmed, and exit to the shell. The display (starting with the current message display) is shown in Fig. 8.17.

Before returning to the shell mail displays the message

        Held 1 message in /usr/spool/mail/troyd

This tells you that one message has been held in your mailbox file.

At the shell prompt, enter

        mail

You should see the header for the remaining message in your mailbox, as shown in Fig. 8.18.

```
?⏎
From troyd Tue Jun  6  09:40 EDT 1989
To: troyd
Subject: test number 2
Status: R

This is the second message that I have sent
to myself!
?⏎
At EOF
?d
?q
Held 1 message in /usr/spool/mail/troyd
$
```

Figure 8.17 Deleting messages in enhanced mail (typical display).

```
$ mail
mail version 2.18 7/1/89.  Type ? for help.
>R   1 troyd      Tue Jun  6 09:31   8/190 test number 1
?
```

Figure 8.18 Messages saved in the mailbox.

NOTE

If, instead of the heading in Fig. 8.18, you received the message: "No mail." you should enter the command

        mail -f

at the shell prompt. Some versions of enhanced mail require the -f option to reread old messages.

Examine the header in Fig. 8.18. Notice that the current message is message number 1 and the status is no longer N (new). At the mail prompt, enter

        d

to delete this message (the > indicates that this is the current message) and then enter

        q

to leave mail and return to the shell prompt.

At the shell prompt, enter the mail command again:

        mail

and you should see the message

        No mail.

since all the messages in the mailbox have been deleted. Your shell prompt should be displayed.

The other commands in Fig. 8.16 are used less frequently. The p command will redisplay the current message. This is useful for long messages that scroll off the screen. To stop the message partway through the output, press your system's interrupt key. The ? command gives you help by listing the mail commands.

This concludes the introduction to enhanced mail.

UNIX commands

mail	read messages from your mailbox
mailx	read messages using enhanced mail (System V)
mail -f	read messages that have been already read but not deleted (required on some versions of enhanced mail)

Mail command mode commands

d	delete the current message
⏎	display the next message
p	display the current message again
q	quit the mail command
s [*file*]	save the current message in the named *file*
?	help; display a list of all mail commands

What Can Go Wrong?

1. After you send a mail message to another user, you later receive a mail message yourself that appears similar to the following message:

```
From troyd Tue Jun 6 08:29:07 1989
Date: Tue, 6 Jun 89 08:28:58 edt
From: MAILER-DAEMON (Mail Delivery Subsystem)
Subject: Returned mail: User unknown
To: troyd
Status: R

 ----- Transcript of session follows -----
550 login-id... User unknown

 ----- Unsent message follows -----
Received: by apsvax.local (1.2/UNIX)
        id AA171151; Tue, 6 Jun 89 08:28:58 edt
Date: Tue, 6 Jun 89 08:28:58 edt
From: troyd (Douglas Troy)
To: troyd
Subject: another message
Cc:

This is another message that I sent to an invalid user
```

Cause: The UNIX mail system could not find the user to whom you tried to send a mail message. You can tell this by looking at the message under the heading ----- `Transcript of session follows` -----. Notice the comment `User unknown`.

Solution: Verify the spelling of the destination login-id when you enter the command `mail` *login-id*. Retry the command with a correct login-id.

2. You have read the messages in your mailbox and you have not deleted them. Later you use the mail command to reread your messages, but you receive the message

```
No mail.
```

Cause: Some versions of mail move messages that have been read into a secondary mailbox file.

Solution: Try using the command

```
mail -f    or    mailx -f
```

to read the messages. If this fails, consult the manuals or use the man command to determine the correct option to read your old messages.

This concludes Chapter 8. At this time you should log off of your UNIX system and review the contents of this chapter by completing the self-test at the end of the chapter.

| Command Summary

UNIX Commands

cd *directory*	change the current working directory
cp *filename pathname*	copy a file to another users directory
cp *pathname filename*	copy a file from another user's directory into your directory
mail	enter mail in command mode to read mail
mail *login-id*	enter mail in send mode to send mail
mailx	enter enhanced mail command mode (System V)
mailx *login-id*	enter enhanced mail to send mail (System V)

mesg [n] [y]	allow and disallow writing to you
who	display who is logged in
write *login-id*	communicate with a logged-in user

Mail Command Mode Commands

d	delete the current message
⏎	display the next message
p	display the current message again
q	quit the mail command
s [*file*]	save the current message in the named *file*
?	help; display a list of all mail commands

Mail Send Mode Commands

Ctrl *and* d	terminate and send the message (A period on a line by itself will also terminate and send the message on many systems.)

Self-Test

1. True or false: The write command is useful only for communicating with users who are currently logged in.

2. True or false: The mail command is useful only for communicating with users who are currently logged in.

3. After composing a mail message, press ___ctrl + d___ to terminate the message and send it to the destination.

4. To send a mail message to the user sallyw, one would begin by entering the command _____.

5. To check to see whether any messages are in your mailbox, enter the command

   _____.

6. The mail command to get help is _____.

7. True or false: You can keep other users from copying files into and out of your home directory.

8. Suppose that you are in mail and you have three messages in the mailbox. If you enter the mail command d, the message that will be deleted is called the _____ message.

9. To keep others from sending messages to you (via the write command), use the _____ command.

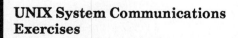

Exercises

1. Log onto your UNIX account. Use the mesg command to disallow messages to your account. Now try to write a message to yourself. Record the message that is displayed by your system.

2. Now, enable writing to yourself using the mesg command and again try to write to yourself. Record the message that is displayed on your screen.

3. Terminate the write session that was initiated in Exercise 2.

4. Use the mail command to send three separate messages to yourself. After sending the messages, delete the second message, but save the other two. Record the commands that you used to perform the above operations.

5. Following Exercise 4, remove the remaining mail messages from your mail box. Record the commands that you used to perform this operation.

9

Making Use of UNIX Multitasking Capabilities

This chapter:

- introduces processes and process management
- describes how to use background processes
- presents the process management commands kill, nohup, and ps

From Chapter 6 you know that when you enter a command at the UNIX shell prompt, the shell searches the directories specified in the search path for a file with the same name as the command. If such a file is found, and if it has execute permissions, then that file contains a program designed to carry out that command. The shell then runs, or executes, that program. (This is true for most commands. A few commands such as cd and set are done by the shell directly. These are called *built-in commands*.)

A program in execution, along with its data, is called a *process* or *task*. This chapter examines the ways in which you can make further use of processes.

Process Status

A primary task performed by the UNIX operating system is to manage **processes**. Every user who is logged into the UNIX system will have a minimum of one process running on his or her behalf: a shell process. Additional processes are created whenever nonbuilt-in commands are executed. Also, many processes are created by the UNIX system itself to aid it in performing its administrative functions. Examples include processes to service the system printer and processes to manage the login requests, plus many others. It is common for a UNIX system to have 50–100 or more processes at a given time.

You can obtain a list of your system's processes by using the **ps** (process status) command. At this time, log into your UNIX system, and enter the command

    ps

This command, without arguments, displays your own processes. The output should be similar to Fig. 9.1a (from System V) or Fig. 9.1b (from a Berkeley system).

This listing states that at the time of the ps command, you had two processes: your shell (sh or csh) and the ps process. The other information in the list is explained in Fig. 9.2.

You will notice that the column labeled STAT, for process *state*, does not appear in the output from some versions of the ps command. Like people, a process goes through various phases called states. People can be in the

```
$ ps
   PID      TTY         TIME         COMMAND
 28887      10          0:02            sh
 29561      10          0:00            ps
 $
```

Figure 9.1(a) Typical output of the ps command on System V.

```
% ps
   PID      TT          STAT  TIME          COMMAND
 28887      p0          S     0:02          -csh (csh)
 29561      p0          R     0:00            ps
 %
```

Figure 9.1(b) Typical output of the ps command on Berkeley version.

160

PID	Process ID. Each process has a unique integer ID number assigned by the UNIX operating system.
TTY	The controlling terminal (workstation) id. This number corresponds to a connection, or port, on the computer.
STAT	Process state. R means running, S means stopped briefly, and I means idle.
TIME	The amount of computer execution time used so far by the process.
COMMAND	The name of the process or program.

Figure 9.2 Meaning of the ps information.

sleeping state, the waiting state, or the working state. Processes, too, can be in various states; for example, executing (running) or waiting for some event such as for data to be read in from a file. All processes go through various states; some versions of the ps command show the state, while others do not.

Look at Fig. 9.3, which is the output from the ps command from a Berkeley version of the UNIX system. Notice that the shell process (csh) is in state S for "stopped" and that the ps process is in state R for "running." The reason that the shell process is stopped is because it is waiting for the ps process to complete. When the ps process is complete, the shell process will resume running and will issue another prompt to the user.

In this example the csh process is called the **parent** process, and ps is considered the **child** process. The shell carries out commands by starting up a child process to perform the command and then waits for the child process to terminate. This is illustrated in Fig. 9.3 by the fact that the csh process is in the stopped state while the ps process is running. System V works in the same way, but the ps command on that system does not show the process state.

Now enter one of the following ps commands, depending on the version of UNIX that you are using:

System V   Berkeley

ps -ae   ps -ax

The a option means *all* processes; the e (for System V) and the x (for Berkeley) means systemwide processes. This command thus requests a

```
% ps
  PID      TT        STAT  TIME       COMMAND
 28887     p0         S    0:02        -csh (csh)
 29561     p0         R    0:00        ps
%
```

Figure 9.3 Typical output of the ps command on Berkeley version.

```
% ps -ax
  PID  TT   STAT   TIME  COMMAND
    0   ?   D      5:10  swapper
    1   ?   I      0:45  init
    2   ?   D      0:01  pagedaemon
   48   ?   IW     0:00  /usr/etc/rwalld
   49   ?   I      3:17  /etc/syslog
   50   ?   S     11:57  /etc/cron
   51   ?   I      2:13  /usr/lib/sendmail -db -qlh -om
18168  p0   S      0:04  -csh (csh)
18169  p0   R      0:01  ps -ax
   51  04   IW     0:00  - auto.9600 tty04 getty
   52  05   IW     0:00  - auto.9600 tty05 getty
            .
            .
            .
%
```

Figure 9.4 Typical abbreviated output from ps -ax (Berkeley version).

listing of all processes running on the system. The output can be extensive. It should resemble Fig. 9.4, which has been abbreviated.

Processes such as *swapper*, *init*, *sendmail*, and *getty* are processes started by UNIX to perform various administrative functions. For example, the *getty* process displays the *login:* message that you see when you log into your UNIX system. Notice also your own processes in the listing; in the case of Fig. 9.4 my processes are csh and ps.

> **Keystroke and Command Summary: Processes status**
>
> UNIX command summary
>
> ps   lists your processes
>
> ps -ax   lists all processes on Berkeley systems
>
> ps -ae   lists all processes on System V

What Can Go Wrong?

1. The commands ps -ae and ps -ax do not list all processes.

Cause: The options on the ps commands can vary on some UNIX systems.

Solution: Use the manual command (man ps) or the printed manuals to find out the options that will list all processes for your system.

Background Processing

You have seen that the shell creates a child process to perform most commands entered by a user. After starting the child process, the shell then waits for the child process to finish running. When the child process is finished, the shell redisplays the prompt and starts the whole sequence over again for the next command.

Time-consuming commands, such as compiling a large program or spell checking a lengthy document, could cause you to sit idle at your workstation while the shell waits for the child process to finish. To avoid these long idle periods, you can tell the shell not to wait for the child process to stop, but instead to redisplay the shell prompt even while the child process is still running. This is called **background processing**. It allows you to enter a time consuming command and, while it is running, go ahead and enter other commands.

To instruct the shell to run a command in the background, you type the & symbol as the last character of the command (just before pressing ⏎). Let's look at an example.

In Chapter 5 we used the following command to list information about launches to Mars, sorted by launch year, from the files "probes.50," "probes.60," and "probes.70":

```
grep Mars probes* | sort -t: +4 > mars
```

Rather than wait for this command to complete, you could run it in the background, allowing you to perform some other task, such as counting the number of launches to Venus, in the foreground. Enter the following commands to demonstrate this. Be sure to include the & as shown to indicate background processing.

```
cd launches
grep Mars probes* | sort -t: +4 > mars&
grep Venus probes* | wc
```

Figures 9.5a (Bourne shell) and 9.5b (C shell) show the results of these commands.

In this example, rather than wait for the first command to complete, the shell returns immediately to the prompt, allowing you to enter the second command. In Figs. 9.5a and 9.5b you will notice that the Bourne shell displays one number after starting the command, while the C shell displays three numbers. These numbers are the Process IDs (PIDs) for the background process(es). The Bourne shell displays the PID for only the last process in the pipeline (sort). The C shell displays the PIDs for all processes (grep and sort) as well as a number in square brackets telling you the number of commands that you currently have in the background.

The C shell notifies you when a background process is complete. The Bourne shell does not. This is also illustrated in Figs. 9.5a and 9.5b. (See the message "[1] Done." in Fig. 9.5b.)

```
$ grep Mars probes* ¦ sort -t: +4 > mars&
1478
$ grep Venus probes* ¦ wc
6          12         198
$
```

Figure 9.5(a)   Background and foreground processing (Bourne shell).

```
% grep Mars probes ¦ sort -t: +4 > mars&
[1]    1511     1512
% grep Venus probes* ¦ wc
6          12         198
[1] Done.
%
```

Figure 9.5(b)   Background and foreground processing (C shell).

You can use the ps command to verify that background processes are running. For purposes of demonstration we will use the sleep command. The syntax is

    sleep *seconds*

For example, the command sleep 5 will simply wait for 5 seconds before terminating. At your shell prompt, enter the commands

    sleep 5&
    ps

and you should see output similar to Fig. 9.6a (Bourne shell) or Fig. 9.6b (C shell).

Notice in Figs. 9.6a and 9.6b that three processes are running: (1) the shell, (2) the sleep process (in the background), and (3) and the ps process in the foreground.

NOTE

We did not use the command from Fig. 9.5 for this example, since that command runs too quickly on many UNIX systems; the command finishes running before the ps command is entered. This is why the sleep command was used: to give you time to enter your ps command. However, any command can be run in the background.

```
$ sleep 5&
2283
$ ps
   PID     TTY   TIME    COMMAND
  2270     T1    0:01    sh
  2283     T1    0:01    sleep
  2284     T1    0:00    ps
$
```

Figure 9.6(a)   Checking background processes with ps (Bourne shell).

```
% sleep 5&
[1] 1511
% ps
   PID    TT   STAT   TIME    COMMAND
  1501    11   S      0:03    -csh (csh)
  1511    11   S      0:00    sleep 5
  1512    11   R      0:00    ps
%
[1]   Done             sleep 5
```

Figure 9.6(b)   Checking background processes with ps (C shell).

> ## Keystroke and Command Summary: Background processes
>
> UNIX command summary
>
> *command*&   the & requests the shell to run the *command* in the background
>
> ps   used to verify that background processes are running
>
> sleep *seconds*   wait *seconds* seconds before returning to the shell

What Can Go Wrong?

1. When you enter the first command shown in Fig. 9.5, you do not see the Process IDs (PIDs) displayed as shown in that figure.

Cause: You did not end the command with the & to indicate background processing.

Solution: Be sure to end the command with the ampersand as shown below:

```
grep Mars probes* ¦ sort -t: +4 > mars&
```

Controlling Processes

Processes that are running in the background can be prematurely terminated (or **killed**) in two ways:

1. by using the UNIX kill command or

2. on System V, if you log off before the process completes.

Consider the **kill** command. The syntax is

```
kill PID
```

where *PID* is the Process ID that is displayed by the shell when you start a background command. The PID is also displayed in the output of the ps command. To demonstrate the kill command, enter the following command (including the &):

```
sleep 10&
```

Notice the PID number that is displayed. Now use that PID in the following command (substitute the number for *PID*):

```
kill PID
```

To verify that the sleep process is terminated, enter the command

```
ps
```

The output from this sequence of commands should resemble Fig. 9.7. (The PIDs will be different on your system.) Notice that the sleep process is not shown in the output from ps because it has been "killed."

System V versions of the UNIX operating system will automatically kill any of your running background processes when you log off. On Berkeley versions of UNIX, background processes will continue to run even if you log off. On System V, if you need to run a process that takes hours (or days) and you can't stay logged on, you can use the **nohup** (no hang up) command

```
% sleep 10&
[1]  20038
% kill 20038
% ps
   PID    TT   STAT  TIME   COMMAND
  20039   11   R     0:00   ps
%
```

Figure 9.7 Using the kill command (Berkeley system).

combined with background processing. For example, the hypothetical command

```
nohup sort huge.file > huge.output&
```

would allow the sort process to continue running even if you log off. For background commands that generate output and run after you log off, it is important to redirect the output into a file, since there will be no workstation screen on which to display the standard output.

> **Keystroke and Command Summary: Controlling processes**
> UNIX command summary
>
> kill *PID*   kill a process with the given Process ID
>
> nohup *command*&   run a background command even if the
>   workstation is logged off

What Can Go Wrong?

1. When you enter the command `kill PID`, the message

```
kill: PID:no such process
```

is displayed

Cause: Either the process with the given PID has already terminated or the PID is incorrect.

Solution: Retry the example in Fig. 9.7 and be sure that you enter the correct PID.

Running a Sequence of Commands

The previous examples have illustrated the use of background processing for a single command. If you need to perform a sequence of commands in the background, use the following command format:

(command 1; command 2; ... command n)&

At the shell prompt, enter the following command:

```
(grep Mars probes* > mars; grep USSR mars > mars.USSR) &
```

This command sequence first creates a file named "mars" with all launches to Mars. Next, the "mars" file is searched for all launches by the USSR. In this example the first command runs to completion before the second command is started.

Unix command summary

(*command 1*; *command 2*; ... *command n*)&

Run a sequence of commands in the background

This completes Chapter 9. Please review the concepts presented in this chapter by completing the self-test at the end of the chapter.

| Command Summary

cd *directory*	change the working directory
command&	the & requests that the command be run in the background
grep *pattern* [*files*]	display lines in a file with the given pattern
kill *PID*	kill a process with the given Process ID
nohup *command*&	run a background command even if the workstation is logged off
ps	list your processes
ps -ax	list all processes on Berkeley systems
ps -ae	list all processes on System V
sleep *seconds*	wait for the indicated number of seconds
(*command 1*; *command 2*; ... *command n*)&	run a sequence of commands in the background

Self-Test

1. The acronym PID stands for _____.
2. When you execute most commands, the shell locates the file that contains the program to carry out the command and runs that program. The shell is called the _____ parent _____ process, and the program is called the _____ process.

3. Compose a command that uses grep to search all three of the "probes" files for launches by the USSR and pipes that information into wc in order to count the number of launches. This command should run in the background:

_____

4. Modify the command in question 3 so that you can log off and the command will still execute: _____

5. Suppose that you have started up a background process that will take a significant amount of time and you realize that you entered the command incorrectly. State the command that you could use to terminate that background command:

_____

6. For question 5, suppose that you forgot to take note of the PID for the background process and the PID has scrolled off your screen. State the command that you could use to determine the PID of your background process: _____

7. True or false: All processes listed by the process status command are in the running state.

Exercises

1. For this exercise you will use the telephone directory file and the phone subdirectory that you created in previous chapter exercises. Write a command that will sort the contents of the file by name, and redirect the sorted output into a file named "phone.sort." Perform this command in the background.

2. Modify the command from Exercise 1 so that it performs a sequence of two separate commands. The first command does the sort as explained above. The second command then prints the contents of the file "phone.sort" on the hardcopy printer. Compose this sequence of commands so that they will run in the background.

3. Modify the sequence of commands in Exercise 2 so that you perform the command "sleep 5" between the sort and print commands. This will give a sequence of three commands. Start this command sequence in the background and then use the ps command to monitor its status.

10

Introduction to UNIX Shell Programming

This chapter:

- further describes operations performed by the shell
- introduces shell procedures
- illustrates the use of shell variables, command line arguments, and built-in commands in procedures
- introduces shell programming with the Bourne shell
- introduces shell programming with the C shell

The purpose of this chapter is to introduce shell programming. The nature of this topic, programming, requires more experience in computing than the topics that compose Chapters 1–9. This chapter is appropriate for readers who have had an introduction to programming using some other programming language.

Operations Provided by the Shell

You know that the UNIX shell is the program that provides many services that assist in performing UNIX commands. Two of these services are standard input and output redirection and expansion of file names using wildcard patterns. As a review, consider the command

```
grep USSR probes* | pr > ussr
```

This command will extract information about launches by the USSR from your "probes" files, paginate this output for a printer, and store the output in a file named "ussr." To perform this command, the shell first expands the wildcard pattern: probes*. Recall that the wildcard character * matches any string of characters. Thus if the current directory contains the files "probes.50," "probes.60," and "probes.70," then the shell will expand the above command to

```
grep USSR probes.50 probes.60 probes.70 | pr > ussr
```

Next, the shell will have to locate and run the tools grep and pr and redirect the standard output of grep into the standard input of pr. The standard output of pr will be redirected into the file "ussr."

The act of accepting commands, determining their meaning, and then acting upon them is called **command interpretation**. This is why the shell is called a **command interpreter**.

But the shell is more than a command interpreter; it is also a *programming language*. The shell allows you to write programs, called **shell procedures**, whose purpose is to control the execution of one or more UNIX commands. You *write* a shell procedure by creating a text file of UNIX commands. You *run* shell procedures by requesting that the shell execute that file of commands. Besides its ability to interpret UNIX commands in a file, the shell language also provides shell variables that permit you to store and pass information between the commands, and it also has certain built-in commands, called **control flow commands**, that allow you to control the order of execution of the UNIX commands in a procedure.

We will begin by looking at the concept of shell procedures. Next, we'll review shell variables and see how they can be used to store and pass information between commands. After this we will look at the shell's control flow commands.

Files of Commands

The simplest application of shell programming is to write a sequence of UNIX commands in a text file and to then have the shell run that shell procedure. Shell procedures are convenient because they allow you to create a file to hold a sequence of commands that you run frequently and later to execute them by using a single command. With procedures you can also create your own UNIX commands.

To see how shell procedures can be useful, go to your UNIX system and log in. At the shell prompt, change the working directory to the "launches" subdirectory by entering

```
cd launches
```

Next, enter vi using the following command. You will now write a shell procedure.

```
vi search
```

The first line of the shell procedure specifies the path name of the shell that will be used to interpret the procedure. This is important, since many UNIX systems have both the Bourne and C shells.

Enter insert mode by pressing

```
i
```

(don't press ⏎). For the Bourne shell, enter

```
#!/bin/sh
```

and press ⏎. For the C shell, enter

```
#!/bin/csh
```

and press ⏎. (*Note:* If your UNIX system has only one shell, this first line is optional.)

Next (for all readers), enter the line

```
grep Mars probes*
```

and press (Esc) to leave insert mode. Recall that this command extracts lines about launches to Mars and displays them on the standard output. Your screen should resemble Fig. 10.1.

Now save the file by entering

```
:wq
```

followed by ⏎. You have just created a simple shell procedure called **search**.

To run the procedure, you set the file's protection mode so that it has execute permissions. (Protection modes were discussed in Chapter 6.) Enter the following command to set the execute permission for the owner:

```
chmod u+x search
```

Now you can run this procedure as a UNIX command. Enter

```
search
```

Figure 10.2 summarizes these two commands and their output.

The shell does not limit you to only one command in a shell procedure; you can have any number of shell commands in a file. This will be illustrated shortly.

```
#!/bin/sh
grep Mars probes*
~
~
~
~
~
~
~
~
~
~
~
~
~
~
~
~
~
~
~
~
~
"search" [New file]
```

Figure 10.1 A simple shell procedure for the Bourne shell. For the C shell, the first line will be #!/bin/csh.

```
$ chmod u+x search
$ search
probes.60:Mariner 4:Mars:US:64
probes.60:Mariner 6:Mars:US:69
probes.70:Mars 2:Mars:USSR:71
probes.70:Mariner 9:Mars:US:71
probes.70:Viking 1:Mars:US:75
$
```

Figure 10.2 Running a shell procedure.

vi *filename*	used here to create a text file of UNIX commands
chmod u+x *filename*	sets execute permissions for the owner for the specified file
#!/bin/sh	first line of a Bourne shell procedure
#!/bin/csh	first line of a C shell procedure

What Can Go Wrong?

1. When you enter the command

```
search
```

the UNIX system displays a message similar to

```
search: Permission denied.
```

Cause: The execute permission is not properly set for the file search.

Solution: Use the chmod command to set the execute permission for the owner (you) by entering the following command at the UNIX prompt

```
chmod u+x search
```

Do not include spaces between the letters u+x.

2. When you enter the command

```
search
```

the UNIX system displays a message similar to

```
search: not found
```

Cause: The first line of the procedure is not correct.
Solution: Be sure the first line is either

```
#!/bin/sh    (for Bourne shell)
```

or

```
#!/bin/csh   (for C shell)
```

174

Shell Variables and Built-in Commands

The search shell procedure illustrated above is not very flexible; it always searches the "probes" files for the same information. It would be more useful if that procedure allowed searches for different information. To do this, we will need to use shell variables.

You have already seen examples of shell variables. These include the variables TERM (Bourne shell), term (C shell), PATH (Bourne shell), and path (C shell). Recall that TERM, or term, is a variable used to hold the name of your terminal type and that PATH, or path, holds a list of directories that the shell searches for commands that you enter.

The shell allows you to associate a value, called a string, with a shell variable. For example, the Bourne shell command

```
TERM=vt100
```

will associate the value vt100 with the variable TERM. The C shell command

```
set term=vt100
```

does the same for the C shell variable named term.

The command used to give a value to a shell variable is called a **built-in shell command** because the shell does this command without running some other program; in other words, these commands are "built in" to the shell itself.

Another built-in command is **echo**. Enter the following command to illustrate the echo command

```
echo my terminal type is $TERM
```

You should see a response similar to

```
my terminal type is vt100
```

although your specific terminal type might be different.

The echo command simply displays (echoes), its arguments to the standard output. In the command in the example above,

```
echo my terminal type is $TERM
```

the arguments are my, terminal, type, is, and $TERM. If an argument is a shell variable (like TERM) and you want to echo the *value* associated with a shell variable, you precede the variable's name with the $ character. Thus $TERM (or $term) means "the value associated with the shell variable TERM (or term)."

You know that many UNIX commands require arguments to specify the object on which the command is to operate. For example, the command

```
cp oldfile newfile
```

uses two arguments. These arguments are called **command line arguments**. Since you run shell procedures like any other UNIX command, they

variable name	contents
$0	the file name of the procedure
$1	first argument value
$2	second argument value
etc.	etc.

Figure 10.3 Predefined shell variables used for command line arguments.

too are permitted to have arguments. To allow a shell procedure to use the command line arguments, the shell automatically associates each argument with a shell variable that can be used inside of a shell procedure. The shell variable names used for the arguments are shown in Fig. 10.3. These are called **predefined shell variables** because the shell itself gives them their meaning.

To illustrate the use of arguments in procedures, we will modify the *search* procedure so that the object to be searched for is entered as a command line argument. Enter the command

```
vi search
```

Modify the file as follows. With the cursor on the first line of the file, press o (lower case "oh") to insert a new second line. Now enter the following new line:

```
echo Searching for $1 ...
```

Press Esc to leave insert mode. Modify the third line so that it reads

```
grep $1 probes*
```

To do so, move the cursor down one line by pressing j and then move it over the M in "Mars" by pressing h as many times as necessary. Delete "Mars" by pressing d *then* w, press i to enter insert mode, and enter

```
$1
```

followed by a space and then press Esc. Your file should resemble Fig. 10.4.

When the shell interprets the command grep $1 probes*, it will substitute the first command line argument in place of the variable $1 before running the grep command. For example, entering the UNIX command search Venus will result in the grep command being interpreted as grep Venus probes*. This way, the command can be used to search for any word in the "probes" file.

Now save your changes and exit vi by pressing

```
:wq
```

and press ⏎.

At the shell prompt, enter the command

```
search Moon
```

and you should see the output shown in Fig. 10.5.

```
#!/bin/sh
echo Searching for $1 ...
grep $1 probes*
~
~
~
~
~
~
~
~
~
~
~
~
~
~
~
~
~
~
~
~
~
~
"search" [New file]
```

Figure 10.4 Shell procedure using a command line argument, Bourne shell version. C shell versions start with #!/bin/csh.

```
$ search Moon
Searching for Moon ...
probes.50:Pioneer 1:Moon:US:58
probes.50:Pioneer 4:Moon:US:59
probes.50:Lunik 1:Moon:USSR:59
probes.60:Ranger 7:Moon:US:64
probes.60:Pioneer 6:Moon:US:65
probes.60:Surveyor 1:Moon:US:66
probes.60:Lunar Orbiter 2:Moon:US:66
probes.60:Luna 13:Moon:USSR:66
probes.60:Surveyor 5:Moon:US:67
probes.60:Surveyor 6:Moon:US:67
probes.70:Luna 17:Moon:USSR:70
probes.70:Luna 19:Moon:USSR:71
$_
```

Figure 10.5 Typical output of the search Moon command.

```
$ grep Mars probes*
probes.60:Mariner 4:Mars:US:64
probes.60:Mariner 6:Mars:US:69
probes.70:Mars 2:Mars:USSR:71
probes.70:Mariner 9:Mars:US:71
probes.70:Viking 1:Mars:US:75
$ echo $?
0
$ grep Pluto probes*
$ echo $?
1
$
```

Figure 10.6a Viewing the return value of a UNIX command with the Bourne shell.

```
$ grep Mars probes*
probes.60:Mariner 4:Mars:US:64
probes.60:Mariner 6:Mars:US:69
probes.70:Mars 2:Mars:USSR:71
probes.70:Mariner 9:Mars:US:71
probes.70:Viking 1:Mars:US:75
$ echo $status
0
$ grep Pluto probes*
$ echo $status
1
$
```

Figure 10.6b Viewing the return value of a UNIX command with the C shell.

The shell variables that represent command line arguments are called *predefined shell variables* because the shell itself creates them.

The shell also supplies additional predefined variables used to represent various other values. One especially useful predefined variable is used to hold the **return value** from the last command executed. If you are using the Bourne shell, enter the commands shown in Fig. 10.6a. For C shell users, enter the commands shown in Fig. 10.6b. Compare your output with the appropriate figure.

The commands

        echo $?   (Bourne shell)

and

        echo $status   (C shell)

display the return value of the last UNIX command. The return value is associated with the predefined variable ? for the Bourne shell or status for the C shell. The return value is used by most UNIX commands to indicate "success" or "failure." In Figs. 10.6a and 10.6b, the first grep command returned 0 to indicate that it successfully located lines containing the word Mars. The second grep command returned 1 to indicate that it failed to find lines containing the word Pluto. Later sections of this chapter include examples that use the return value in shell procedures.

Besides the predefined shell variables, you can use your own names as shell variables. This will also be demonstrated shortly.

Keystroke and Command Summary: Shell variables and built-in commands

UNIX (shell) commands

echo *arguments*	display argument values
echo $?	display the return value of the last command for the Bourne shell
echo $status	display the return value of the last command for the C shell
variable=value	associate a value with a shell variable (Bourne shell)
set *variable=value*	associate a value with a shell variable (C shell)

Predefined shell variables

$0	the file name of the procedure
$1	first argument value
$2	second argument value
.	.
.	.
.	.
$?	return value of the last command (Bourne shell)
$status	return value of last command (C shell)

What Can Go Wrong?

1. When you enter the command

```
search Moon
```

the command does not display any launch information.

Cause: In the shell procedure, did you include the $ on the predefined shell variable in the procedure? Did you spell Moon with an uppercase M?

Solution: Be sure to enter the grep command as

```
grep $1 probes*
```

Don't put a space between the s in "probes" and the *.

The examples above have demonstrated that shell procedures consist of a sequence of UNIX commands and may also utilize shell variables. The shell also provides built-in commands that allow procedures to be written so that the UNIX commands are interpreted repetitively (in loops) and/or conditionally. These kinds of commands are called **control flow commands** because they control the flow of execution of the UNIX commands in a shell procedure.

One of the major differences between the Bourne shell and the C shell is in the syntax of the control flow commands. Because of this, the next section is written in two versions: one for the Bourne shell and another for the C shell. Read the section that is appropriate for your use.

Control Flow: Bourne Shell

Conditional Command

Conditional commands are sometimes called "if" commands. They provide control so that a command can be either interpreted or skipped on the basis of some condition. The syntaxes for the Bourne shell conditional commands are shown in Figs. 10.7a and 10.7b.

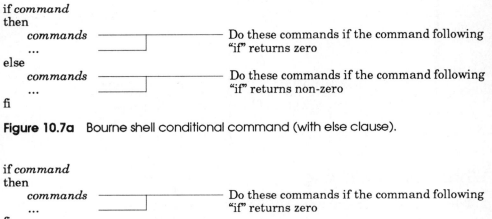

```
if command
then
        commands ──────────────┐  Do these commands if the command following
        ...           ─────────┘  "if" returns zero
else
        commands ──────────────┐  Do these commands if the command following
        ...           ─────────┘  "if" returns non-zero
fi
```

Figure 10.7a Bourne shell conditional command (with else clause).

```
if command
then
        commands ──────────────┐  Do these commands if the command following
        ...           ─────────┘  "if" returns zero
fi
```

Figure 10.7b Bourne shell conditional command (without else clause).

Look at Figs. 10.7a and 10.7b. The words then, else, and fi form "blocks" of commands that are conditionally executed. In Figure 10.7a the block of commands between then and else are executed only if the command following if is zero (true); otherwise, the block between else and fi is executed. Figure 10.7b shows that the else clause is optional. In this if command, the shell interprets the command following the if and then executes the "then" block only if that command returns zero (true). Let's use this command in our search procedure.

Recall the search procedure:

```
#!/bin/sh
echo Searching for $1 ...
grep $1 probes*
```

This command would be more user-friendly if it displayed a diagnostic message if no information was found by the grep command. For example, if the user entered search Pluto, the command could display the message No launch information about Pluto. Let's do this.

We saw in the previous section that the grep command returns zero to indicate success (that is, it finds one or more matches) or 1 if it fails to find a match. To check the return value in an if command, the shell provides the built-in command **test**. The syntax of test is

test *expression*

The test command evaluates the expression to see whether it is true or false. If the expression is true, then test returns the value zero, otherwise, it returns a nonzero value.

The test command has its own syntax for the expression. Two of the expressions allowed by the test command are shown in Fig. 10.8. The symbols = and != (entered as ! *then* =) are **logical operators**. The = tests for equality, and != tests for nonequality.

Let's use the if and test commands. Using vi, edit your search procedure by entering

vi search

Modify the file so that it contains the commands shown in Fig. 10.9. Be sure to put the words then and fi on lines by themselves; this is one of the syntax rules.

string1 = *string2*	true if *string1* and *string2* are identical
string1 != *string2*	true if *string1* and *string2* are not identical

Figure 10.8 Some expressions for the test command.

```
#!/bin/sh
echo Searching for $1 ...
grep $1 probes*
if test $? != 0
then
      echo No launch information about $1
fi
```

Figure 10.9 Search procedure with a conditional command.

If you need help remembering a vi command, refer to Appendix A. Notice how the commands between then and fi are indented. This is a style convention that makes the control flow of the procedure easier to follow. When you have finished editing, enter

   :wq ⏎

to save your file.

Now, test the procedure by entering the commands shown in Fig. 10.10. Your output should resemble that shown in the figure.

Keystroke and Command Summary: Conditional command
Bourne shell commands

if *command*   conditionally interpret blocks of commands
then
     commands
     ...

```
$ search Mars
Searching for Mars ...
probes.60:Mariner 4:Mars:US:64
probes.60:Mariner 6:Mars:US:69
probes.70:Mars 2:Mars:USSR:71
probes.70:Mariner 9:Mars:US:71
probes.70:Viking 1:Mars:US:75
$ search Neptune
Searching for Neptune ...
No launch information about Neptune
$_
```

Figure 10.10 Testing the conditional command.

```
    else
        commands
        ...
    fi
    if command
    then
        commands
        ...
    fi
```

What Can Go Wrong?

1. When you enter the command

```
Search Mars
```

you receive a message similar to

```
search: syntax error at line 9: 'fi' unexpected
```

Cause: You did not put the word then on a line by itself, or you have made some other syntax error in your if command.

Solution: Review your procedure and be sure that it corresponds to Fig. 10.9. Use vi to make any needed changes and again try to run the procedure.

2. When you enter the command

```
Search Mars
```

you see the output from the grep command followed by a message similar to one of the following

```
search: test: unknown operator ?
```

or

```
search: test: argument expected
```

or some other message that includes *test:*.

Cause: There is a syntax error in the test command's expression.

Solution: Be sure that you do not have any spaces between the symbols in the $? and the !=. Be sure that there are spaces as shown below:

```
if test $? != 0
|   |  | |                          Spaces here
```

Review Fig. 10.9 and make any necessary changes to your procedure and try again to run the procedure.

3. When you ran the search command, you received output from the grep command that included not only the "probes" files but also the "allprobes" file.

Cause: In the line grep $1 probes* you included a space between the s and the *.

Solution: Use vi to remove the extra space. Save the new procedure and test it again.

Iteration Commands

Iteration commands, sometimes called **looping commands**, allow you to repeat the execution of one or more commands. An example of how iteration might be used is to execute the shell procedure for each command line argument. This would allow a single command like search Moon Mars Jupiter to search for information about all three planets.

We will examine two of the Bourne shell's iteration commands: for and while. Their syntaxes are shown in Figs. 10.11 and 10.12.

Notice that in both the for and while commands, the words do and done form a block of commands that are under the control of those statements.

The **for** command works by giving the shell variable *name* the value *word1*, then interprets all commands in its block. It then gives the shell variable *name* the value *word2* and again interprets all of the commands in

```
for name [ in word1 [word2 ...] ]
do
      commands
      ...
done
```

Figure 10.11 The for command.

```
while command
do
      commands
      ...
done
```

Figure 10.12 The while command.

the block. It repeats this procedure for each of the words listed in the for part of the statement. An example of a for command is the following:

```
for planet in Moon Mars Venus
do
     echo Searching for $planet
     grep $planet probes*
done
```

This for command will do the echo and grep commands three times: once with the shell variable planet given the value Moon, the second time given the value Mars, and the third time given the value Venus. In this example the shell variable *planet* is called a **user-defined shell variable**.

To interpret the **while** command, the shell interprets the command after the while. If the command's return value is zero, it interprets its associated block of commands. It then goes back and again interprets the command after the while. If that command returns zero, the block of commands is again interpreted. This action is repeated as long as the while command returns zero.

To modify the search procedure so that it will search for more than one command line argument, you need to use another predefined shell variable along with the for command. When the predefined shell variable

```
$*
```

is interpreted by the shell, it is replaced with a list of *all* of the command line arguments. Thus the built-in shell command

```
for planet in $*
```

would be expanded by the shell to

```
for planet in Moon Mars Venus
```

when its shell procedure is started with the command

```
search Moon Mars Venus
```

Let's try the for command. Using vi, modify your search procedure so that it contains the commands given in Fig. 10.13. Notice that the commands between do and done are all indented. This is a style convention that makes the flow of control easier to follow. After you have finished editing, save the file and exit from vi.

Test the modified procedure by entering

```
search Moon Mars Pluto Saturn
```

Your output should resemble Fig. 10.14.

```
#!/bin/sh
for planet in $*
do
    echo Searching for $planet ...
    grep $planet probes*
    if test $? != 0
    then
        echo No launch information about $planet
    fi
done
```

Figure 10.13   Using the for command.

```
$ search Moon Mars Pluto Saturn
Searching for Moon ...
probes.50:Pioneer 1:Moon:US:58
probes.50:Pioneer 4:Moon:US:59
probes.50:Lunik 1:Moon:USSR:59
probes.60:Ranger 7:Moon:US:64
probes.60:Pioneer 6:Moon:US:65
probes.60:Surveyor 1:Moon:US:66
probes.60:Lunar Orbiter 2:Moon:US:66
probes.60:Luna 13:Moon:USSR:66
probes.60:Surveyor 5:Moon:US:67
probes.60:Surveyor 6:Moon:US:67
probes.70:Luna 17:Moon:USSR:70
probes.70:Luna 19:Moon:USSR:71
Searching for Mars ...
probes.60:Mariner 4:Mars:US:64
probes.60:Mariner 6:Mars:US:69
probes.70:Mars 2:Mars:USSR:71
probes.70:Mariner 9:Mars:US:71
probes.70:Viking 1:Mars:US:75
Searching for Pluto ...
No launch information about Pluto
Searching for Saturn ...
probes.70:Voyager 2:Jupiter,Saturn:US:77
probes.70:Voyager 1:Jupiter,Saturn,Uranus:US:77
$
```

Figure 10.14   Output from the search procedure with the for command.

What Can Go Wrong?

1. When you enter the command

```
search Moon Mars Pluto Saturn
```

you see the following (or similar) message displayed:

```
search: syntax error at line 3: 'echo' unexpected
```

Cause: You did not put the word do on a line by itself, or you have made some other syntax error in your for command.

Solution: Review Fig. 10.13. Make any necessary corrections to your procedure and try again to run it.

2. When you enter the command

```
search Moon Mars Pluto Saturn
```

you do not receive the expected output.

Cause: You have mistyped a shell variable name.

Solution: Be sure all shell variables are entered correctly. Check both $* and $planet.

Case Command

A final built-in shell command that will be introduced in this section is called the **case** command. It is actually a conditional command and is a convenience for use when you would be required to use several if commands in sequence

```
          case string in
             pattern) commands ;;
             pattern) commands ;;
             ...
          esac
```

Figure 10.15 The case command.

that test the same result. The syntax for the case command is shown in Fig. 10.15.

The case command works by comparing the string to each of the patterns. For the first pattern that matches the string the shell then interprets the commands that follow, up until the two semicolons. Control then passes to the next command after the esac. If the string matches none of the patterns, then none of the commands are interpreted. The patterns consist of strings that may contain wildcard symbols. Let's look at an example.

At the shell prompt, enter the command

```
date
```

and you should see a line similar to the following:

```
Fri Jun 5 13:20:34 EST 1989
```

Now enter the command

```
today=`date`
```

Notice that the ` symbol is the **grave accent**, also called the **back quote**. Notice also that there are *no spaces* around the equals sign. This command will take the result of the date command and associate it with the shell variable today. (Today is a user-defined shell variable.) To verify this, enter

```
echo $today
```

and you should see the date and time displayed.

Now we will use this command along with the case command to write a procedure that will remind you of tasks to be accomplished each day. Create a new file by entering the command

```
vi tickler
```

and enter the following text into that file:

```
#!/bin/sh
echo For today:
today=`date`
case $today in
     M*)   echo Do progress report ;;
     Tu*)  echo Arrange car pool ;;
     W*)   echo Half way to weekend
           echo Project meeting today!
           ;;
```

```
        Th*)  echo Run diagnostics of computer ;;
        F*)   echo Ready for weekend! ;;
    esac
```

Save the file and exit from vi. This procedure uses the case statement to select one set of five messages to be displayed, depending on the day of the work week. Notice the use of the * wildcard symbol in the case command's patterns. The pattern M* will match any string that begins with uppercase M. In particular, any value for $today that begins with M will match that pattern. Note also that each case can have more than one command; each case ends with the double semicolon.

To test the procedure, change the mode of the tickler file to executable by entering the following command at the shell prompt:

```
    chmod u+x tickler
```

and then enter the command

```
    tickler
```

You should see one of the five messages displayed, assuming that the day on which you are doing this tutorial is one of the days of the work week. If the day is Saturday or Sunday, none of the five tickler messages will be displayed.

> **Keystroke and Command Summary: Case command**
>
> Bourne shell commands
>
> *name=`command`*   interpret the *command*; associate the
>   result with the shell variable *name*
>
> case *string* in
>
>   *pattern*) *commands* ;;
>
>   *pattern*) *commands* ;;
>
>   ...
>
> esac

What Can Go Wrong?

1. When you enter the command

```
    echo $today
```

the result is the word

```
    date
```

instead of today's date and time.

Cause: When entering the command

```
today=`date`
```

you did not enclose the word date in grave accent characters (back quotes).

Solution: Enter

```
today=`date`
echo $today
```

Use grave accents. Do not use any spaces around the equals sign.

2. When you enter the command

```
tickler
```

the UNIX system displays a message similar to

```
tickler: not found
```

Cause: You incorrectly entered the first line of the procedure.

Solution: Be sure that the first line of the procedure is

```
#!/bin/sh
```

3. When you enter the command

```
tickler
```

the UNIX system displays a message similar to

```
tickler: Permission denied.
```

Cause: The execute permission is not properly set for the file tickler.

Solution: Use the chmod command to set the execute permission for the owner (you) by entering the following command at the UNIX prompt:

```
chmod u+x tickler
```

Don't include spaces between the letters u+x.

4. When you enter the command

```
tickler
```

you see a message similar to

```
tickler: syntax error at line 5: ) unexpected
```

Cause: You have a missing ;; after one of your echo commands.

Solution: Review the example in the text. Be sure to include the double semicolons after each case. Make any necessary corrections with the editor and try the procedure again.

5. When you enter the command

```
tickler
```

you see a message similar to

```
tickler: syntax error at line 13: 'end of file' unexpected
```

Cause: The esac command is missing, or it is not on a line by itself.

Solution: Review the example in the text. Make any necessary corrections with the editor and try the procedure again.

This completes the introduction to the Bourne shell's control flow statements. If you are not interested in reading about the C shell, you should now log off of your system and review the chapter by completing the self-test at the end of the chapter.

Control Flow: C Shell

Conditional Command

Conditional commands are sometimes called "if" commands. They provide control so that a command can be either interpreted or skipped on the basis of some condition. The simplified syntax for the C shell conditional commands are shown in Figs. 10.16a and 10.16b.

The *"expression"* after the if in Figs.s 10.16a and 10.16b can be either a UNIX command or a logical expression. Logical expressions are used to

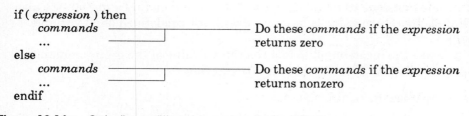

```
if ( expression ) then
    commands ───────────────────  Do these commands if the expression
    ...                            returns zero
else
    commands ───────────────────  Do these commands if the expression
    ...                            returns nonzero
endif
```

Figure 10.16a C shell conditional command (simplified).

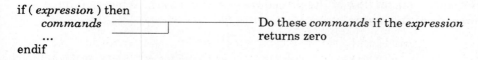

```
if ( expression ) then
    commands ───────────────────  Do these commands if the expression
    ...                            returns zero
endif
```

Figure 10.16b C shell conditional command (without else clause).

compare two values together. Two examples of logical expressions are as follows:

Expression	Meaning
string1 == *string2*	0 (true) if *string1* is identical to *string2*, nonzero (false) otherwise
string1 != *string2*	0 (true) if *string1* is not identical to *string2*, nonzero (false) otherwise

The symbols == (= *then* =) and != (! *then* =) are called **logical operators**. They are used to compare two values.

Look at Figs. 10.16a and 10.16b. The words then, else, and endif form "blocks" of commands that are conditionally executed. In Fig. 10.16a the block of commands between then and else are executed only if the expression following if is zero (true), otherwise, the block between else and endif is executed. Figure 10.16b shows that the else clause is optional. In this if command, the shell interprets the expression following the if and then executes the "then" block only if that expression is zero (true). Let's use this command in our search procedure.

Recall the search procedure:

```
#!/bin/csh
echo Searching for $1 ...
grep $1 probes*
```

This command would be more user-friendly if it displayed a diagnostic message if no information was found by the grep command. For example, if the user entered search Pluto, the command could display the message No launch information about Pluto. Let's do this.

We saw previously that the grep command returns zero to indicate success (that is, it finds one or more matches) or 1 if it fails to find a match. We also saw that the return value is associated with the predefined shell variable *status*.

Let's use the if command to test the return value of the grep command. Using vi, edit your search procedure by entering

```
vi search
```

Modify the file so it contains the commands shown in Fig. 10.17. (If you need help remembering a vi command, refer to Appendix A.) Notice how the commands between then and if are indented. This is a style convention that makes the control flow of the procedure easier to follow. When you have finished editing, enter

```
:wq ⏎
```

to save your file.

```
#!/bin/csh
echo Searching for $1 ...
grep $1 probes*
if ( $status != 0 ) then
    echo No launch information about $1
endif
```

Figure 10.17 Search procedure with a conditional command.

Now test the procedure by entering the commands shown in Fig. 10.18.
Your output should resemble that shown in the figure.

> **Keystroke and Command Summary: Conditional command**
>
> C shell commands
>
> if (*expression*) then
>   *commands*
>
>   ...
> else
>   *commands*
>
>   ...
> endif
>
>
> if (*expression*) then
>   *commands*
>
>   ...
> endif

```
% search Mars
Searching for Mars ...
probes.60:Mariner 4:Mars:US:64
probes.60:Mariner 6:Mars:US:69
probes.70:Mars 2:Mars:USSR:71
probes.70:Mariner 9:Mars:US:71
probes.70:Viking 1:Mars:US:75
% search Neptune
No launch information about Neptune
%
```

Figure 10.18 Testing the conditional command.

What Can Go Wrong?

1. When you enter the command

```
search Mars
```

you see a message similar to

```
search: permission denied
```

Cause: The file protection mode does not include execute permission.

Solution: At the UNIX prompt, enter

```
chmod u+x search
```

Then retry the search command.

2. When you enter the command

```
search Mars
```

you see a message similar to

```
search: syntax error at line 2: ( unexpected
```

Cause: You did not include the line

```
#!/bin/csh
```

as the first line of your procedure. Your login shell may be the C shell, yet your system may use the Bourne shell as the default for interpreting shell procedures. You must include the csh path as indicated above to override the default.

Solution: Use vi to enter that line at the top of the file.

3. When you enter the command

```
Search Mars
```

you see the output shown Fig. 10.18 with the additional line

```
if: Empty if.
```

Cause: The word then is missing from the if command.

Solution: Review your procedure and be sure that it corresponds to Fig. 10.17. Use vi to make any needed changes and again try to run the procedure.

4. When you enter the command

```
search Mars
```

you receive the output shown in Fig. 10.18 with the additional line

```
then: then/endif not found.
```

Cause: The word endif is missing from the procedure.

Solution: Review Fig. 10.9 and make any necessary changes to your procedure and try again to run the procedure.

5. When you enter the command

```
search Mars
```

your system displays the output shown in Fig. 10.10 but also includes one of the following messages:

```
No launch information about Mars
```

or

```
if: Expression syntax
```

Cause: The expression: $status != 0 is entered incorrectly.

Solution: Review the if command in Fig. 10.9. Be sure that there are *no* spaces between the ! and the = characters in the expression. There *should be* a space before the ! and after the =. Use vi to make any necessary corrections and retest the procedure.

Iteration Commands

Iteration commands, sometimes called **looping commands,** allow you to repeat the execution of one or more commands. An example of how iteration might be used is to execute the shell procedure for each command line argument. This would allow a single command like search Moon Mars Jupiter to search for information about all three planets.

The C shell provides two iteration commands: foreach and while. Their syntaxes are shown in Figs. 10.19 and 10.20.

```
foreach name ( word1 [word2 ...] )
    commands
    ...
end
```

Figure 10.19   The foreach command.

```
while ( expression )
    commands
    ...
end
```

Figure 10.20   The while command.

Notice that in the **foreach** command the words foreach and end enclose a "block" of commands that are interpreted under the control of that statement. In the while command the words while and end enclose the block.

The foreach command works by giving the shell variable *name* the value *word1*, then interprets all commands in its block. It then gives the shell variable *name* the value *word2* and again interprets all of the commands in the block. It repeats this procedure for each of the words listed in parentheses. An example of a foreach command is the following:

```
foreach planet ( Moon Mars Venus )
    echo Searching for $planet
    grep $planet probes*
end
```

This foreach command will do the echo and grep commands three times: once with the shell variable planet given the value Moon, the second time given the value Mars, and the third time given the value Venus. In this example the shell variable *planet* is called a **user-defined shell variable**.

To interpret the **while** command, the shell interprets the expression enclosed in parentheses. If the expression has the value zero (true), then the shell interprets its associated block of commands. The shell then goes back and again interprets the expression. If that expression still has the value zero, then the block of commands is again interpreted. This action is repeated while the expression has the value zero (that is, true).

To modify the search procedure so that it will search for more than one command line argument, you need to use another predefined shell variable along with the foreach command. When the predefined shell variable

```
$*
```

is interpreted by the shell, it is replaced with a list of *all* of the command line arguments. Thus the built-in shell command

```
foreach planet ( $* )
```

would be expanded by the shell to

```
foreach planet ( Moon Mars Venus )
```

when its shell procedure is started with the command

```
search Moon Mars Venus
```

Let's try the foreach command. Using vi, modify your search procedure so that it contains the commands given in Fig. 10.21.

Notice that the commands between foreach and end are all indented. This is a style convention that makes flow of control easier to follow. After you have finished editing, save the file and exit from vi.

```
#!/bin/csh
foreach planet ( $* )
  echo Searching for $planet ...
  grep $planet probes*
  if ( $status != 0 ) then
     echo No launch information about $planet
  endif
end
```

Figure 10.21   Using the foreach command.

Test the modified procedure by entering

    search Moon Mars Pluto Saturn

Your output should resemble Fig. 10.22

```
$ search Moon Mars Pluto Saturn
Searching for Moon ...
probes.50:Pioneer 1:Moon:US:58
probes.50:Pioneer 4:Moon:US:59
probes.50:Lunik 1:Moon:USSR:59
probes.60:Ranger 7:Moon:US:64
probes.60:Pioneer 6:Moon:US:65
probes.60:Surveyor 1:Moon:US:66
probes.60:Lunar Orbiter 2:Moon:US:66
probes.60:Luna 13:Moon:USSR:66
probes.60:Surveyor 5:Moon:US:67
probes.60:Surveyor 6:Moon:US:67
probes.70:Luna 17:Moon:USSR:70
probes.70:Luna 19:Moon:USSR:71
Searching for Mars ...
probes.60:Mariner 4:Mars:US:64
probes.60:Mariner 6:Mars:US:69
probes.70:Mars 2:Mars:USSR:71
probes.70:Mariner 9:Mars:US:71
probes.70:Viking 1:Mars:US:75
Searching for Pluto ...
No launch information about Pluto
Searching for Saturn ...
probes.70:Voyager 2:Jupiter,Saturn:US:77
probes.70:Voyager 1:Jupiter,Saturn,Uranus:US:77
$
```

Figure 10.22   Output from the search procedure with the foreach command.

What Can Go Wrong?

1. When you enter the command

    search Moon Mars Pluto Saturn

you see the following (or another line beginning with foreach:) displayed:

    foreach: Too few arguments

Cause: The foreach command is incorrectly entered. Did you include the parentheses shown in Fig. 10.21?

Solution: Review Fig. 10.21. Make any necessary corrections to your procedure and try again to run it.

2. When you enter the command

    search Moon Mars Pluto Saturn

you do not receive the expected output.

Cause: You have mistyped a shell variable name.

Solution: Be sure all shell variables are entered correctly. Check both $* and $planet.

Switch Command

A final built-in shell command that will be introduced in this section is called the **switch** command. It is actually a conditional command and is a convenience for use when you would be required to use several if commands in sequence that test the same result. The syntax for the switch command is shown in Fig. 10.23.

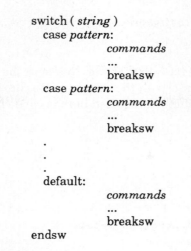

```
        switch ( string )
           case pattern:
                      commands
                      ...
                      breaksw
           case pattern:
                      commands
                      ...
                      breaksw

             .
             .
             .

        default:
                      commands
                      ...
                      breaksw
        endsw
```

Figure 10.23 The switch command.

The switch command works by comparing the string to each of the patterns. For the first pattern that matches the string the shell will then interpret the commands that follow that pattern, up until the command breaksw.
Control then passes to the next command after the endsw. If the word
matches none of the patterns, then the commands following the word default:
are interpreted. If the default case is not included and there are no matches,
then none of the commands in the switch are interpreted. The patterns
consist of strings that can contain wildcard symbols. Notice that the *case
pattern*: parts of the command are on a line by themselves. Let's look at an
example.

At the shell prompt, enter the command

```
date
```

and you should see a line similar to the following:

```
Fri Jun 5 13:20:34 EST 1989
```

Now enter the command

```
set today='date'
```

Notice that the ' symbol is the **grave accent**, also called the **back quote**.
Be sure not to put any spaces around the equals sign. This command will
take the result of the date command and associate it with the shell variable
today. (Today is a user-defined shell variable.) To verify this, enter

```
echo $today
```

and you should see the date and time displayed.

Now we will use this command along with the switch command to write a
procedure that will remind you of tasks to be accomplished each day. Create a

new file by entering the command

```
vi tickler
```

and enter the following text into that file. Notice in the switch command that the word $today is enclosed with the double quote character (the " is a single keystroke). The double quote is required here because the value of $today contains spaces.

```
#!/bin/csh
echo For today:
set today=`date`
switch ( "$today" )
      case M*:
              echo Do progress report
              breaksw
      case Tu*:
              echo Arrange car pool
              breaksw
      case W*:
              echo Half way to weekend
              echo Project meeting today!
              breaksw
      case Th*:
              echo Run diagnostics of computer
              breaksw
      case F*:
              echo Ready for weekend!
              breaksw
endsw
```

Save the file and exit from vi. This procedure uses the switch statement to select one set of five messages to be displayed, depending on the day of the work week. Notice the use of the * wildcard symbol in the case command's patterns. The pattern M* will match any string that begins with uppercase M. In particular, any value for $today that begins with M will match that pattern. Notice also that each case can contain one or more commands; the breaksw command ends each case.

To test the procedure, change the mode of the tickler file to executable by entering the following command at the shell prompt:

```
chmod u+x tickler
```

and then enter the command

```
tickler
```

You should see one of the five messages displayed, assuming that the day on which you are doing this tutorial is one of the days of the work week. If the day is Saturday or Sunday, none of the five tickler messages will be displayed because the default case is not included in this example.

> **Keystroke and Command Summary: Switch command**
>
> set *name*= `command`   interpret the *command*; take the result and associated it with the shell variable *name*
>
> switch (*string*)
>   case *pattern*:
>
>   *commands*
>   ...
>   breaksw
>
>   case *pattern*:
>
>   *commands*
>   ...
>   breaksw
>
>   .
>   .
>   .
>
>   default:
>
>   *commands*
>   ...
>   breaksw
>
> endsw

What Can Go Wrong?

1. When you enter the command

```
echo $today
```

the result is the word

```
date
```

instead of today's date and time.

  Cause: When entering the command

```
set today='date'
```

you did not enclose the word date in grave accent characters (back quotes).

  Solution: Enter

```
set today='date'
echo $today
```

Use grave accents. Do not use any spaces around the equals sign.

2. When you enter the command

```
tickler
```

the UNIX system displays a message similar to

```
tickler: not found
```

Cause: You incorrectly entered the first line of the procedure.

Solution: Be sure that the first line of the procedure is

```
#!/bin/csh
```

3. When you enter the command

```
tickler
```

the UNIX system displays a message similar to

```
tickler: Permission denied.
```

Cause: The execute permission is not properly set for the file tickler.

Solution: Use the chmod command to set the execute permission for the owner (you) by entering the following command at the UNIX prompt:

```
chmod u+x tickler
```

Don't include spaces between the letters u+x.

4. When you enter the command

```
tickler
```

you see a message similar to

```
Syntax error.
```

Cause: You have a typing error somewhere in your switch command. For example, this error could be caused if in the switch command the word $today is not enclosed in double quotes.

Solution: Review the example in the text. Make any necessary corrections with the editor and try the procedure again.

5. When you enter the command

```
tickler
```

you see a message for the appropriate day of the week, followed by messages for the rest of the workdays.

Cause: The breaksw command is missing from one or more of your cases. Without the breaksw command, control will "fall into" the next case.

Solution: Review the example in the text. Make any necessary corrections with the editor and try the procedure again.

This completes the introduction to the C shell's control flow statements. At this time you should log off of your UNIX system and review your understanding of the material by completing the self-test at the end of the chapter.

| Command Summary

UNIX Commands

cd *directory*	change the working directory
chmod u+x *filename*	set execute permissions for the owner for the specified file
echo *arguments*	display argument values
grep *pattern* [*files*]	display lines that match the pattern
variable=value	associate a value with a shell variable (Bourne shell)
set *variable=value*	associate a value with a shell variable (C shell)
test *expression*	evaluate a conditional expression
vi *filename*	used here to create a text file of UNIX commands

Predefined Shell Variables

$0	the file name of the procedure
$1	first argument value
$2	second argument value
.	.
.	.
.	.
$*	all command line arguments
$?	the return value of the last command (Bourne shell)
$status	the return value of the last command (C shell)

Shell Commands: Conditional and Iteration

Bourne Shell: see pages 180, 184, and 188

C Shell: see pages 191, 195, and 199

Self-Test

1. The shell is both a command _____ and a _____.

2. A file of shell commands is called a shell ___procedure___

3. To display the value of the shell variable HOME, one could use the following echo command: _____ echo $HOME

4. A shell variable that is automatically given a value by the shell is called a ___predefined___ shell variable.

5. For your shell, state the name of the shell variable that corresponds to the following contents:

   Variable   *Contents*

   a. _$?_   Return value of the last program

   b. _$2_   The second command line argument

6. The following is an incomplete command that will echo the value of all of the command line arguments. Complete the command by filling in the blanks. Use the command appropriate for your shell.

   for arg in _$*_   foreach arg (____)

   do   echo _____

        echo _arg_   end

   done

7. Compose the command that can be used to set the execute permissions for the owner for the file named "doit": ___chmod u+x doit___

8. Consider the following incomplete shell procedures (Bourne and C shell versions):

   wc allprobes   wc allprobes

   if test _$? -0_   if (_____) then

   then   echo _____

        echo _file not found_ endif

   fi

   For your shell, complete the procedure so that it outputs the message File not found if the wc command fails. Use the usual return value for a successful command.

9. The command

   ```
   who am i
   ```

   will return a line of information about your own login-id and UNIX connection. For your shell, compose a command that will associate the result of this command with the shell variable named me: ___set me = `who`___

10. Consider the following sequence of if commands:

Bourne shell:

```
if test $choice = A
then
        echo A is not correct
fi
if test $choice = B
then
     echo B is not correct
fi
if test $choice = C
then
     echo C is correct!
fi
```

C shell:

```
if ( $choice == A ) then
     echo A is not correct
endif
if ( $choice == B ) then
     echo B is not correct
endif
if ( $choice == C ) then
     echo C is correct!
endif
```

For your shell, rewrite the above sequence of if commands using either a case or a switch command.

Exercises

1. For this exercise you will use the telephone directory file and the phone subdirectory that you created in previous chapter exercises. Write a shell procedure that will search for a name in your telephone directory. Allow the name to be entered as a command line argument.

2. Modify the shell procedure from Exercise 1 so that if no name is found, the message "That person is not in the directory" is displayed on the screen. You must use the shell's if command to check the return value from the grep command.

3. Modify the shell procedure from Exercise 2 so that you can enter a list of one or more names on the command line. You should use the $* predefined shell variable and the "for" or "foreach" commands. For each name that is not found, display the message from Exercise 2, but substitute the actual name in place of the words "That person."

Command Summaries

vi Command Summary

Starting vi:

vi *filename*	create or edit a file
vi -r *file*	recover an edit session

Leaving vi:

:wq ⏎	save changes and quit
:q! ⏎	quit without saving changes

Saving and reading files:

:w ⏎	save changes and return to editing
:w *filename* ⏎	write changes to a new filename
:r *filename* ⏎	read the text from the file into the current file

Cursor movement:

j	* down a line
h	* left one character
l	* right one character
k	* up one line
0	move to beginning of current line
$	move to end of current line
H	move to beginning of current window (not

* indicates commands that can be preceded by a number to indicate repetition. For example, 6dd will delete six lines.

	covered in the text)
L	move to last line of current window (not covered in the text)

Inserting text:

a	append after cursor
A	append to end of current line
i	insert before cursor
I	insert at beginning of current line
o	open a new line below the current line
O	open a new line above the current line

Paging through text:

Ctrl *and* b	back one screen
Ctrl *and* d	down a partial screen
Ctrl *and* f	forward one screen
Ctrl *and* u	up a partial screen
G	go to end of file
*n*G	go to line number *n*

Searching through text:

/*string* ⏎	search forward for the string
?*string* ⏎	search backward for the string
n	repeat the previous search forward
N	repeat the previous search backward
:[*start,end*]s/*old text*/*new text*/⏎	substitute the *new text* for the *old text* for lines *start* through *end*. If start and end are skipped, substitute on the current line only. Using 1 for start and $ for end includes all lines in the file

Changing text:

x	* delete a character
dw	* delete a word
dd	* delete a line
D	delete to end of line
J	join current line and the next line (not covered in the text)
r	replace current character
R	replace text to end of line (not covered in the text)
u	undo previous command

Copying and moving text:

Y	* yank a line, or lines, into the buffer
yy	* same as Y
yw	* yank a word into the buffer (not covered in the text)
dd	* delete a line, or lines, and save them in the buffer
p	put lines from the buffer below the cursor
P	put lines from the buffer above the cursor

UNIX Command Summary

Shell Commands   Page

command < *file*	redirect the standard input from file	79
command > *file*	redirect standard output to file	79

command >> *file*	redirect standard output, append to file	79
command1 ¦ *command2*	pipe standard output of *command1* into *command2*	79
command&	run the command in the background	163
(*command1*; *command2*)&	run the sequence of commands in the background	167
Ctrl *and* d	terminates the shell; also log off command	15

(See pp. 204–205 for a summary of control flow commands.)

Predefined Shell Variables   Page

$0	command name	176
$1	first command line argument	176
$2	second command line argument	176
$*n*	*n*th command line argument	176
$?	return value of last command (Bourne shell)	178
$status	return value of last command (C shell)	178
$*	all command line arguments	185, 196
$#	the number of command line arguments (Bourne shell) (not described in the text)	

Shell Wildcard Characters   Page

*	matches any string of characters	71
?	matches a single character	71
[*characters*]	matches a set of characters or a range (e.g., [1–9])	71

UNIX Commands   Page

apropos *topic*	find commands about a topic	91
cat [*files*]	concatenate and display files	77
cd [*directory*]	change directory	66
cd ..	change directory to the parent directory	67
chmod *who op pathname*	change file or directory permissions	100
cp *oldfile newfile*	copy files	64
csh	C shell	161
date	display current date and time	188, 199
echo *arguments*	output arguments	108
ed [*file*]	line-oriented text editor	29
exit	logoff command for some systems	15
export *variable*	make the shell variable available to other commands (Bourne shell)	24
grep *pattern* [*files*]	search files for a pattern	83
help *topic*	another name for apropos on some systems	91
kill PID	terminate a process	166
lp [-d*printer*] [*filenames*]	print specified files on system printer	36
lpr [-d*printer*] [*filenames*]	print specified files on system printer	36
lprint [*filenames*]	print on a locally attached printer	37
logout	logoff command for some systems	15

Answers to Chapter Self-Tests

Chapter 1

1. make the computer easier to use; manage the computer system's resources
2. a. single-user interactive
   b. multitasking (or multiuser)
   c. real time
   d. time sharing
3. program development; text processing
4. time sharing, multiuser
5. False
6. shell
7. kernel
8. False
9. portability
10. b, c, e, and f

Chapter 2

1. False
2. passwd
3. This is system dependent. The UNIX default is @ *then* ⏎.

4. True
5. This is system dependent. The UNIX default is Ctrl *and* d. Other logout commands are exit and logout.
6. Bourne shell and C shell.
7. shell
8. This is system dependent. Typical interrupt commands are Del or Ctrl *and* c.
9. editor
10. insert; command
11. True
12. directory
13. ls
14. cat
15. This is system dependent. Possibilities are lp, lpr, and lprint.
16. set

Chapter 3

1. a. dd
   b. x

c. i
d. a
e. (Esc)
f. k
g. j
h. :
i. O
j. o
k. u
2. i, a, O, o
3. u
4. r

Chapter 4

1. a. mkdir homework
   b. cp lab1 homework   or
      cp lab1 homework/lab1
   c. cp lab1 oldlab1
   d. mv oldlab1 homework   or
      mv oldlab1 homework/oldlab1
   e. cd homework
   f. pwd
   g. rm oldlab1
   h. cd ..
2. /etc/passwd
3. root
4. a. This is system dependent.
      Examples are:
      lp *5   or   lpr *5   or   lprint *5
   b. ls s???
   c. rm *.o
   d. cat *[1-9]
5. This is system dependent; 14 or 256
   is typical.
6. ii

Chapter 5

1. standard output device; standard
   input device
2. filter
3. a. |
   b. >
   c. >>
   d. <
4. apropos (or help on some UNIX systems)
5. The command is system dependent
   and based on the command used to
   print a file. Examples include:

man grep | lpr
man grep | lp
man grep | lprint

6. The pr command paginates for hard
   copy. The command is
   man grep | pr
7. Assuming that "probes.50,"
   "probes.60," and "probes.70" are the
   only files in the current directory
   that match the wildcard probes.*,
   then the following command could
   be used:
   grep USSR probes.*
   The command:
   grep USSR probes.50 probes.60
   probes.70
   would also work.
8. Pipe the output into wc. For example:
   grep USSR probes.* | wc
   (The three individual file names
   could be listed in place of the
   wildcard file name.)
9. grep Venus probes.* | sort -t: +3 -4
   (The three individual file names
   could be listed in place of the
   wildcard file name.)
10. grep Venus probes.* | sort -t: +3 -4
    probes.* > venus
11. This is system dependent and
    based on the command used to
    paginate to the screen. Possibilites
    are:
    cat probes.* | more
    cat probes.* | pg

Chapter 6

1. a. ls -la
   b. ls -ld launches
   c. chmod go-x .
   d. chmod ug+x myfile
   e. cd
   f. cd ..
   g. This is system dependent. Use:
      PS1="-->"   for the Bourne shell
      or
      set prompt="-->"   for the C shell
2. a. rwx, read/write/execute
   b. ---, none
   c. 32567 bytes
   d. root

e. cfit

f. no, because the first character of the permissions is not d

3. For the Bourne shell: .profile
   For the C shell: .login

4. the current directory

5. echo $TERM

6. search path

Chapter 7

1. i, a, I, A, o, O

2. dw and 8x

3. a. /Saturn
   b. ?Sun
   c. 1G
   d. A
   e. G

4. 0 (zero) and 6h

5. j, 2dd, G, p

6. j, 2Y, G, p

7. yank

8. :1,$s/:7/:197/ ⏎

9. :w probes.new ⏎, :q! ⏎

10. :r probes.70 ⏎

11. False. (Change to the directory where the crash occurred and start vi with the -r option.)

12. :r, :w, :q, :q!, /, ?,
    :s/old text/new text/ (substitute)

Chapter 8

1. True

2. False

3. Ctrl and d
   (Many versions of mail also allow: .
   then ⏎ on a line by itself.)

4. mail sallyw (or mailx sallyw when using enhanced mail on System V)

5. mail (or mailx when using enhanced mail on System V)

6. ?

7. True

8. current

9. mesg n

Chapter 9

1. Process ID

2. parent, child

3. grep USSR probes* ¦ wc&

4. For Berkeley systems, no change is needed (nohup is assumed). For System V: nohup grep USSR

probes* ¦ wc&

5. kill

6. ps

7. False

Chapter 10

1. interpreter, programming language

2. procedure

3. echo $HOME

4. predefined

5. a. For Bourne shell: $?
      For C shell: $status
   b. $2

6. for arg in $*   foreach arg ($*)
   do   echo $arg
        echo $arg   end
   done

7. chmod u+x doit

8. wc allprobes
   if test $? != 0
   then
        echo File not found
   fi
   or
   wc allprobes
   if ($status != 0) then
        echo File not found
   endif

9. For Bourne shell: me=`date`
   For C shell: set me=`date`

10. For Bourne shell:
    case $choice in
         A) echo A is not correct ;;
         B) echo B is not correct ;;
         C) echo C is correct! ;;
    esac
    For C shell:
    switch ("$choice")
         case A:
              echo A is not correct
              breaksw
         case B:
              echo B is not correct
              breaksw
         case C:
              echo C is correct!
              breaksw
    endsw
    (Note: In this case "$choice" does not need to be enclosed in parentheses.)

Index